Influence

adamstones.co/influence

To Sylvia and Noah, my love and purpose

BIS Publishers
Borneostraat 80-A
1094 CP Amsterdam
The Netherlands
T +31 (0)20 515 02 30
bis@bispublishers.com
www.bispublishers.com

ISBN 978 90 6369 611 5

Design and layout by Ivica Jandrijević
Illustrations by Elena Brighittini
Copy edited by Manda Waller
Special thanks for invaluable support: Gareth Jones (The Drawing
Board) and Peter Gilheany (Forster Communications)

adamstones.co/influence

Influence

/ Powerful
communications

/ Positive
change

Adam Stones

/Preface

If you want to change the world, how do you get the world on board?

When I moved to Amsterdam from London in 2016, my first impressions were of a city buzzing with the spirit of entrepreneurialism. Everywhere I went, I encountered people powered by a purpose to bring about positive social and environmental change, whether it was through a community movement, a new venture, scientific research or a consumer innovation. Whatever your line of work or interest, there seemed to be plenty of areas to apply your passions. And that gave me so much excitement and hope.

However, I soon noticed something was holding these changemakers back. There was so much purpose but, for many, there was a lack of clear communications. They were struggling to tell me the core of their ideas, as well as how they planned to get these ideas out into the world. Some didn't know who their audiences really were or what they were *really* offering them. And if they couldn't explain it to me, how did they expect to convince their colleagues, customers, campaigners or collaborators? (Warning: this book contains an enthusiastic use of alliteration...)

I found that although support might be readily available on how to access investors or business mentorship (for example), often the information on how to communicate effectively was confusing, fragmented or just not there. And I realised that if this was happening in Amsterdam, then changemakers in less socially conscious communities must have to contend with far more challenges. As I dug deeper, I started to understand the scale of the enterprises, movements and individuals around the world which are failing to reach their full potential – or simply failing – because of this.

So I used my background in big communications agencies and newsrooms to help build the communications functions of start-ups and scale-ups, as well as the skills of individuals, through consulting, capacity-building and training workshops. And this work has been exclusively with people committed to positive social or environmental change. Brand development, media strategies, content production, public speaking and pitching... the essential communications attributes of leaders. I've been working to show that these can all be learned quickly and mastered with a little commitment, by anyone.

As Covid hit and nurseries closed, I had to pause this work to focus on looking after my young son. With more time to spend on teaching him how to build Lego towers (or rather smash mine over), take his first steps and knock the local ducks on the head with stale bread, I realised with a growing conviction that my rising anxiety over the world he is entering could be reduced by other educational actions. I felt that if I could pass on some of my communications knowledge to a wider audience then I might help contribute to democratising communications for social good. I outlined the idea for this book and sent it to BIS publishers, knowing there was no single book out there that covered all these essential ingredients. I told them: 'It is my firm belief that tooling up changemakers to become better communicators – and thereby increasing their influence – can help change the world.' I am incredibly grateful that they agreed.

But what does it take to achieve influence?

That's what we're here to find out.

/What's Inside

///
//////////////////////////// **Welcome 8**

Learn the communications secrets of leaders and how you will apply these, using the canvas that accompanies this book.

///
///////// **Step 1: Be purposeful 20**

Start your journey to Influence by finding out how purpose drives your life (and your success), uncovering your own authentic purpose and exploring how to create meaningful action from it.

///
////////// **Step 2: Be personal 32**

Who is the target for this purpose? And who will help you make it happen? All your communications start by knowing in detail who your audiences are and how to connect with them.

///
/////////// **Step 3: Be distinct 50**

What are you offering these audiences? Learn what a brand really is and how you can build one that covers everything on the inside and outside – whether that's a personal or organisational brand.

//
//////////////// Step 4: Be active 86

Before you bring this brand to life, we need to dive into the science and psychology of how we will change your audience's attitudes and actions. With this knowledge, we'll produce a plan for the year ahead and discover how to check your progress.

//
///////////// Step 5: Be Skilled 120

Your plan will come alive when you have the skills to deliver it:

/**BODY LANGUAGE** 122

/**PERSUASIVE CONVERSATIONS** 130

/**KILLER CONTENT** 144

/**STORYTELLING** 158

/**WRITING** 168

/**PR & MEDIA** 184

/**PUBLIC SPEAKING** 198

//
/////////////////////// Onwards 216

The world needs you and your passion so, armed with the knowledge and tools from this book, let's get to work.

WELCO

Archimedes – he of the overflowing bath fame – said, 'Give me a lever long enough and I will move the world.' Powerful communication provides that lever by giving you influence and, in this book, we're going on a journey to find out how to push it. **First up, we'll decode the 'Five traits of influence', which we see in all inspiring communicators (spoiler alert: these traits are also the names of the next five chapters).** We'll then look at how to use the unique, accompanying Influence Canvas to plot your progress. **We'll finish this opening chapter by setting a clear intention for your future success.** Eureka.

/HOW TO INFLUENCE

When we witness a powerful communicator, something magical happens. Their idea takes hold of us. We feel excited as that idea grows inside us and we start to nurture it. They haven't just shared information, they have planted a seed and, with that, they have fundamentally changed our beliefs and future actions.

Picture Martin Luther King telling us of the dream that then becomes *our* dream. Or Greta Thunberg's climate activism that inspires us to change our own ways. Or Malala Yousafzai's passionate advocacy for education that fills us with outrage and empathy. Great communicators connect with us, stir our emotions and lead us on a new path.

It is not being an influential leader that has made these people great communicators, but just the opposite. It is a powerful command of communications disciplines and skills that has enabled them to lead. You simply can't be a leader of change until you are a powerful communicator, and that applies whether you wish to lead a movement, a purposeful organisation or a game-changing new product out into the world.

Great communicators affect us whether they are on stage, in person or in an article. They are found in every field, at every level of an organisation. They are defined by their behaviour not their job title, by their promise of the future not by their past.

Apple was right in its 'Think different' philosophy when it said 'Here's to the misfits, the rebels, the troublemakers', because it's the people who are bold enough to *think* they can change the world that actually *do*. It's the ones that 'think different' who inspire us to 'do different'.

And that doesn't always mean having wholly original ideas – it can also mean just picking up something we already know to be true and taking charge of it, and leading people behind that idea in a new way. In fact, one of your principal jobs as a leader is to make the new feel inviting and the familiar feel exciting.

Getting people to 'do different' will take some work. But it's within your grasp. Every single leader in history – politically, philosophically and religiously – has become a leader through not only having beliefs but also by having the ability to tolerate and navigate the hard work and hurdles it takes to bring people over to a new way of thinking. You are – either in a big or small way – the same.

From communicating to connecting

In a fair world, the ideas that can accelerate positive social or environmental impact would be the ones that shine out, get shared and acted on. It should be easy, right? You should be able to say, 'Check out my great idea to make your life a LOT better,' and wait for people to line up to sign up. Alas, instead, we live in a paradox.

Throughout the day we will have multiple conversations, send dozens of emails, make social posts and broadcast all sorts of messages through our beautiful body language. Anyone can quickly create a website, share a video or even just shout their beliefs out of their window if they wish (hello to my noisy neighbour, if you're reading this). In short, it's never been easier to communicate. And yet it's also never been harder to connect. There is so much information out there that we are always competing to be heard. And we often end up just adding to the noise.

As a result, many people are struggling to cut through and communicate effectively. And poor communications is a recurring theme of failure or conflict in business, politics, society and even everyday life (including in our relationships). With poor communications, we will confuse, remove someone's desire to act and – at worst – encourage advocates against our ideas.

Using the example of small businesses: in the USA, the Small Business Administration organisation found in 2019 that about 20% of business start-ups fail in the first year and about 50% within five years (and Covid will of course make those stats even more grim in future). One of the top five reasons identified for failure was poor communications. And we see the same picture of communication-led failure within individual enterprises, non-profits and social movements.

But despite the difficulties, some people do manage to get attention, to be heard and lead people to change. How do they do this?

The 5 Traits of Influence

I have studied a range of individuals and organisations in depth to find out what makes them such powerful communicators – what enables them to influence – and I've decoded all these attributes into five core traits that every successful leader deploys to navigate the communications paradox.

These five traits are:

Purposeful: They are driven by a bigger cause with a clear vision for a more positive future. And they make their passion for this *our* passion also.

Personal: They single us out with an empathetic understanding of who we are, even in a crowd. Their message is not about them but about what it can do for us. They are supported by a tribe of advocates and an army of collaborators.

Distinct: They have a consistent, recognisable profile and a clear message that is easy to understand. We know what we will get from them each time and we understand the value of their unique contribution.

Active: They back up their words with impactful actions, built on their deep knowledge of how change really happens. They are seen in diverse, influential places. They aren't afraid to learn from mistakes.

Skilled: They have conviction and confidence, informed by their competence across a range of essential communications skills, from persuasive conversations and public speaking to writing, storytelling and handling the media.

With these traits, they inspire us, they influence us. They don't tell us what to do, they make us want to do it. These traits are, by their dictionary definition, *the determining qualities or characteristics* of these powerful communicators. And all of these traits need to be embraced, developed and applied *collectively* if you want to have the greatest chance of success yourself. I've done the hard work for you in identifying this formula and now I'm sharing it with you in a way that is accessible and easy for you to apply.

How to use this book and its canvas

This book has been structured to guide you through these five traits, step by step, over the next five chapters. I'm inviting you to pause, reflect and rebuild your approach to communications. You will learn the techniques that have been tried and tested by the best, as well as how to use these however you choose to communicate, whether that's in person, on stage, broadcast, in print or online. This knowledge is universal – it is not specific to any sector or country and sits outside and above communications trends, to give you something that will serve you for years to come.

We'll identify your purpose, find your audiences, build your brand, form a communications plan and develop your core skills. You can jump into the book at any point, especially if you have a skill you need to build right now (Got a TED talk coming up? No problem, skip to page 198), but I recommend starting at the start, as a unique value of this book is how it will help you to build up the knowledge completely, layer by layer.

Throughout the book, you'll find real-world examples and a bunch of practical insights from other experts. These inputs are from individuals, of course, but also from big business, social movements and community groups (which I will refer to collectively for ease as 'organisations'). As individuals, we can learn a great deal from such organisations. The principles *they* apply are the same ones *we* should. And because their work plays out on bigger stages, often the lessons are more clear to see.

In each chapter, you will also find summaries of the key points. You can use these to get a quick refresher when you need a top-up or for instant advice when on the go. This is a book that's meant to be *used,* not just *read.* I hope you will have folded corners, and cookie crumbs and coffee stains on the pages as you write, plot and get going. This book is designed to be your personal communications coach, replacing having me in the room (which, given the state of me after many months of lockdown and Lego is no bad thing, let me assure you).

Accompanying this book is the unique Influence Canvas that I have designed specifically to help you capture all the key insights and plans you identify as you progress through the five traits. It's a stripped-back version of the book, in once place. At the end, with your canvas complete, you will have something to pin on your wall and guide your communications efforts for the year ahead. It's your bird's eye, practical view of how you will achieve influence. (Just watch out for where I've listed 'Canvas Action' through the book and I'll explain what you need to fill in.)

Please take a second now to look over the canvas on page 18. You can download a more detailed template – with guidance – from my website at adamstones.co/influence, where you'll also find a range of other tools and resources.

Who is this book for?

So if you're reading this, you're one of those changemakers I mentioned in the preface. But what else? An entrepreneur, a campaigner, a rebel, a disruptor? All of the above? Many of you may have got here because you are already successful as engineers, educators, designers, inventors or many other things, and suddenly find you now also need to be an expert at communications if you want to move upwards, with more impact. You may be the founder of a fast-growth SME, with investors interrogating your value and impact. You might be a solo consultant who needs to convince the world that your ideas deserve attention. You might be looking to find your voice as a leader as you grow your movement for social or environmental justice. Or you might be a professional, within a larger organisation, who wants to take the next step up the ladder, and for whom great communication skills will set you apart.

Influence is here to help all of you. It is aimed primarily at individuals, but in a way that you can use it to either further your own personal capacity as a leader or to progress an organisation by creating and then leading its communications activities – as the process I lay out can be used either way. I've designed it to help anyone who wants to bring about change – anyone with an idea, mission or movement for a more positive future – whether you have dreams of turning the world on its axis or just making your part of it a little bit better.

I spoke with Impact Hub and Ashoka, two of the biggest international organisations championing social entrepreneurs and societal changemakers, respectively. Both agreed that change is driven by powerful communications.

'ALL OF US ARE BORN WITH A DREAM TO MAKE THE WORLD A BETTER PLACE. LEARNING TO COMMUNICATE THAT DREAM IS WHAT WILL MAKE THE WORLD A BETTER PLACE.'

– NANCY DUARTE, *RESONATE*

Tatiana Glad, co-founder of Impact Hub Amsterdam, said: 'For some entrepreneurs, communications is still seen as an extra cost or something they can tag on later. But it should be factored in from the start and should be understood for the considerable value it provides. It is tempting to want to jump straight into productisation, securing investors or sales, for example, but successful entrepreneurs understand the role communications has in helping to facilitate all those things. To be taken seriously, you have to take communications seriously.'

Martina Zelt of Ashoka agreed: 'If you want to activate people to contribute to solving the many challenges in our world today, you need to find a common language; practice empathy and communicate well. Only then can your vision spread. Powerful communication and changemaking are inseparable from one another.'

Successful communicators get noticed. By showing clarity and vision in the face of an uncertain future, you will create more demand – and societal value – for yourself and your ideas. You'll start to enjoy bigger stages for your message; more high-profile media opportunities and speaking events. This all results in better contacts, better clients, better jobs – all aligned with your values. It will lead to more success in pitches, more chances of a promotion, more sales, more members or easier recruitment. Whatever you're working on, it will help you to achieve your ambitions.

So, what is the success you are looking for?

Time to set your intention

Committing to being a powerful communicator is also committing to taking more control over your life. Before we proceed and learn about communications, you must first set your intention for how you will use your influence. This is different to the change you want to see in the world (we'll get to that next...). This is about the change you want to see in yourself. Essentially, why did you pick up this book? It was probably a feeling. Now let's turn that into something concrete.

Perhaps you want to power up your communications to take your organisation to new heights, or to take yourself to more commanding places. Picture the future you, armed with the skills of powerful communications. What are you doing? Your intention – your goal – could be 12 months ahead or five years. Capture that picture, whatever and wherever it is. We'll use it to keep you on track and motivate you, through this book and beyond.

///

CANVAS ACTION: This is your first entry. Kick off your canvas by writing your intention at the top, completing the sentence 'I will use my influence to...'. Now say to yourself, 'I will do this.'

///

Name:

Intention:

PURPOSEFUL	My purpose			
PERSONAL	Primary audiences		Secondary audiences	
DISTINCT	Vision	Values / Behaviours	Essence & Value Proposition	
	Mission			
	Archetype / Character		Thought Leadership	
ACTIVE	Objectives / Plan summarised	Commitments	Channels (OSEP)	
SKILLED	Skill audit			

Your Influence Canvas

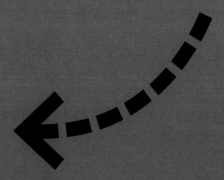

1 PURF

OSEFUL

Your purpose is powerful. It's your drive for bringing about change. It's your reason for getting out of bed in the morning. **It's what gives your life meaning, affirms your identity and shapes your goals.** It should be the basis for every decision you make and every message you convey. **And, quite simply, it's vital to your ability to influence. But have you ever actually written down what it is?** Let's start by exploring your purpose and how we'll use it to establish a foundation for meaningful action and powerful communications.

/YOUR
PURPOSE

As we look at all the fun things happening around us – climate breakdown, insectageddon, plastic oceans, toxic air, social rifts, oh and pandemics – it is understandable that we should be expecting (with ever-increasing demand) everyone to step in and step up to help. Anxiety over the world around us is leading to distrust in everything from the systems that we live by to the people and organisations that maintain those systems. And this distrust is leading to disruptive innovation.

We are increasingly looking to connect with the movements that can accelerate this disruption, we want to support the organisations that are also demanding more and we want to follow the people that can guide us through this to something better beyond. Purpose takes you from managing to mobilising. It gives people hope. Sustainability has been a key term for some years now – but this will not be enough for much longer: we need regeneration. Simply, the time for identifying and sharing how you're going to lead the way in the new world is now.

There are a number of groups driving this increasing demand for purpose, including:

Customers (otherwise known as 'everyone'): Meaningful Brands found that three-quarters of worldwide consumers expect brands to contribute to their well-being and quality of life. (Note: as we'll discuss later – *you* are a brand).

Employees: Danone UK found that a quarter of British managers would take a pay cut for a purpose-led job, and half would leave if their company's values and purpose did not align with their own.

Investors: Larry Fink, CEO of Blackrock, the world's largest investment company said, 'Without a sense of purpose, no company, either public or private, can achieve its full potential. It will ultimately lose the license to operate from key stakeholders.'

These stats relate primarily to businesses, but the same picture is reflected in the voluntary and public sector. Change is being driven by demand from both outside and within. And the message from all angles is clear: **find your purpose or find the exit**. Those that put purpose at their heart demonstrably outperform those that don't. They last longer. They achieve their ambitions.

Looking at some of the great communicators from the previous chapter, like Malala Yousafzai or Martin Luther King, you can see that being driven by something much bigger than yourself – and being able to communicate what that is – is integral to making people believe in you. Because, when you centre everything in *why* you do things, it is truly inspiring; it can win fans, build communities and start movements. As Simon Sinek says in his famous TED talk, **'People don't buy *what* you do, they buy *why* you do it'**, so you must start there.

'IF ONE MAN CAN DESTROY EVERYTHING, WHY CAN'T ONE GIRL CHANGE IT?'
– MALALA YOUSAFZAI, *I AM MALALA*

So, what do you stand for? What is driving the change you want to create? As you're reading this particular book, chances are you're driven by some bigger purpose and may even already be taking action on this. But have you properly *articulated* your purpose or do you just *know* it in your heart? Are your actions and communications *rooted* in your purpose or do they just instinctively *feel* right?

Identifying your purpose

There is no one-size-fits-all when it comes to finding purpose. It can range from the **epic** – such as helping to progress the UN's Sustainable Development Goals – to the **everyday,** giving your audiences opportunities to find such things as happiness, human connections or empowerment. And it can either be **founding** (where your work was established to create a positive impact) or **found** (where a positive connection has been established later, to give a valuable new focus).

Whatever you do and wherever you do it, you might try to use the diagram on the facing page: **purpose is the intersection where your passions and skills overlap with what the world needs**. It is within this magic centre that you find true meaning and can apply the most energy. And by using this model you will identify a purpose that is genuine and relatable. It gives you a great story to tell about why you do what you do. My own purpose – using my passion and skills for communications and writing to help changemakers – fits perfectly in that centre. Even though there may be a few other things I 'do', it is this which drives me forward and provides the filter through which I run my decisions. It was this model that helped me to identify the opportunity to write this book.

When I shared this model on LinkedIn, people responded really positively. One person also told me it was very similar to a model that interprets the Japanese idea of Ikigai, which is about leading a good everyday life. But in that model, there is a fourth overlapping circle included, for financial reward, ensuring that your purpose is also what you get paid for. You can add that if you want, but I personally believe that if you commit to applying your passions and skills in areas that the world needs then that will be rewarded in itself; either

What the world needs

What your passions are

What you're great at

P

financially or otherwise. And for some of you, of course, money is not an intended outcome of what you are working on.

If it helps to steer your thinking, innovation company IDEO has defined five ways that your purpose could have an impact on the world. You can test these out and see where you find most alignment. (Search for 'Purpose Wheel' at ideo.com to see the full tool.) In summary, the five ways are:

Reduce Friction: Simplifying and eliminating barriers by creating relief, giving control or unlocking freedom.

Foster Prosperity: Supporting the success of others by providing security, lending support or offering nourishment.

Encourage Exploration: Championing discovery by cultivating connections, inspiring curiosity or celebrating creativity.

Kindle Happiness: Inciting joy by nurturing inclusion, spreading wonder or instilling pride.

Enable Potential: Inspiring greater possibilities by empowering growth, championing education or pioneering transformation.

Examples of organisations / individuals in these categories, in order, might include: Amnesty International / Seth Godin, Oxfam / Michelle Obama, AirBnB / David Attenborough, Dove / Oprah Winfrey, Nike / Malala Yousafzai.

Clearly there are many ways you can make a difference, and it is very possible your own purpose could have elements of more than one type. Use my tool and / or IDEO's as guides to steer your thinking and then capture more detail beneath the headline this helps you find. Once you have done this, check it is genuine by asking if you will be able to support your intentions with your actions. But also ensure it will challenge you a little – you need this to trigger excitement and incite motivation.

I'm not going to list a bunch of example purpose statements to guide your thinking, as everyone does it differently and I'd like you to create something unique and authentic, from your heart. (Fear not, there will be *plenty* of practical examples for all the other influence traits we will be building later.) It will also be your choice if you even state your purpose publicly – many people choose not to, and keep it as a personal guide. And in a later chapter we'll be looking at how we expand on this purpose statement to construct the brand that *will* be our external showcase. But first... action.

///

CANVAS ACTION: Produce a short statement that captures *your* purpose, and add it to the canvas.

///

From purpose to action

Once the purpose has been established it *must* be lived. That means brought to life with authentic action. You cannot communicate about your purpose externally until it exists everywhere internally. It must live through the culture and operations of what you do, then find its way into products, services and experiences. Only then can you consider external communications. But even then, you should be telling the stories of the action your purpose is leading to, rather than the belief itself. There is no point saying you care about something if you are doing nothing. And in these difficult times, there is arguably no greater opportunity to express authentic action against your purpose.

A name often associated with purpose is Patagonia. When Yvon Chouinard founded the outdoor clothing company to help people explore wild places, he concluded it should also be in the business of protecting wild places. As Patagonia says, '**We appreciate that all life on earth is under threat of extinction. We're using the resources we have – our**

business, our investments, our voice and our imaginations – to do something about it.' That philosophy has driven every decision the company takes, and the actions that embody this grow every year.

Already donating a share of its profits to causes fighting for the environment, in 2019 it launched Patagonia Action Works, a digital platform to allow its customers to directly connect with and support the thousands of organisations it champions. And in 2020, ahead of the US Presidential election, it started using its clothing tags to display provocative messages like 'Vote the assholes out'. You can probably guess who it was referencing. Patagonia's actions are effective because they are communicated with credible personality and because, by enabling and empowering its customers as advocates of their purpose, the ideas get shared and implemented many times more.

For anyone concerned that purpose must always be massive, that you need to always be like Patagonia, be assured – you can start with the small stuff. And once you have started, it is easy to imagine how the small seeds could grow. Let's say your start-up sells reusable water bottles. It could be positioned initially as helping people to take action on plastic waste. Later, when confidence and influence grow, you might take action as a brand with beach clean-ups (inviting your audiences to join in), open-call design challenges (around using recycled ocean plastic in your products) and forming partnerships with other sustainability change agents to create communities around the issues you care about – and maybe even address policies and systems change. Suddenly the engagement, support and reach of your purpose *is* massive.

Purpose washing and virtue signalling

Some people try to jump straight to the action bit, without taking the time to explore what is really driving them, and without defining the

find your
PURPOSE

or find the
EXIT

difference they can make. Worse, the power of purpose to attract others to a brand is so compelling it's causing people and brands to try and signal purpose in their communications while doing nothing to live it. You may have seen the advert where Kendall Jenner offers a can of Pepsi to a police officer at the head of a protest march and suddenly the tension dissolves and everyone loves each other. The ad was met with widespread condemnation that the drinks giant was appropriating – even trivialising – the Black Lives Matter movement. The ad was pulled and Pepsi's reputation was rightly mauled.

In 2020, many organisations *visually* supported Black Lives Matter but did nothing to support the cause. Their empty statements suggested that black lives only matter to them when there's profit to be made. And many organisations are doing the same 'purpose washing' with causes related to the environment, gay rights, indigenous rights and more. But where this happens, thankfully there are many millions of people waiting to call them to account.

An authentic purpose establishes trust. And 'establishing trust' also happens to be one of the key objectives of communications. But fail to live up to the purpose promise and the disconnect kills that trust. Take Facebook – Zuckerberg says 'it was built to accomplish a social mission, to make the world more connected,' but the UK's Digital, Culture, Media and Sport select committee says the way the company leveraged those connections for its own financial gain through data harvesting makes them nothing short of 'digital gangsters'. Decreasing trust results in diminished performance – even diminishing funding – and also means communications efforts are directed at putting out fires, rather than furthering ambitions.

People powered by purpose are more energised to achieve great things and are hugely more attractive to their audiences. They will be the only survivors in this new era of consciousness. In fact, they will be the ones that define what this new era looks like.

/PURPOSEFUL SUMMARY

THE POWER OF PURPOSE: Consumers, employers and funders are all calling for individuals and organisations to find their purpose to help solve the world's social and environmental challenges. The door is open for you.

IKIGAI: You can find your true purpose at the sweet spot intersection of your passions and skills, and what the world needs.

YOUR CONTRIBUTION: Going further, use IDEO's model to help define the impact of your purpose. Its five suggested areas are: Reduce friction, Foster prosperity, Encourage exploration, Kindle happiness and Enable potential.

FROM EVERYDAY TO EPIC: Some people are activating their purpose on epic scales, addressing systemic challenges like the SDGs. But you could choose to address epic issues in small ways or even address everyday issues. Once you start, it's easy to see how your commitment to your purpose can build.

LIVE IT: With your purpose defined, it must be lived in every part of your or your organisation's DNA, steering decisions. Live it internally before taking it externally.

TAKE ACTION: You now have opportunities to take authentic, meaningful, impactful action. By following these steps and being genuine, you avoid being accused of purpose washing. And instead of having to defend your reputation, you build trust and advocates, and you create change. This action – this change you're leading – gives you something important to talk about. More on this over the coming chapters.

RSONAL

There's a wise old saying (that I might have made up): 'You wouldn't send a letter without first putting a name and address on the envelope.' Well, duh, but it is an important maxim for communications. **You can't expect your message for change to arrive at its destination if you don't know – *really* know – who you're speaking to or how it's going to reach them.** Before we build your brand, and before we come up with some clever tactics for activating it, we first need to understand who you are doing all that for and how you can connect with them. **Let's get personal with your audience.**

/FIND YOUR AUDIENCES

It is tempting – and much easier – to try and appeal to everyone. But by doing that you end up connecting with no one. How can you be *personal* if you don't know the person? We've already started to cast our minds into the future to explore your intention and purpose. So let's look around there a bit more – who do you see? Who are you influencing? Who has helped you to get there? Essentially, who are the individuals, groups and communities that you need to *act* in order to help further your purpose?

Take a moment now to make a long list of *all* the audience types that come to mind. Depending on your work, the groups you identify might include some of these:

Customers Volunteers Beneficiaries Influencers Employees Funders Delivery partners Membership organisations Retailers Conference organisers Manufacturers Academic institutions Activists Politicians Researchers Government bodies NGOs

When you have your list, it might be quite long. Scanning across the names, you can see that you obviously won't send the same type of message or ask the same action of all these groups, nor can you actually communicate with all of them anyway. There's just too many. We need to focus our attention, so next we prioritise.

Let's split your groups into **primary audiences** (the main focuses of your change messages) and **secondary audiences** (the organisations and individuals who support you and may also communicate with your primary audiences on your behalf – often referred to as our **stakeholders**). Here's how...

Primary audiences

Most of the time you will have one primary audience – one focus for your key messages – and that's likely to be your customer. But sometimes you may have two, such as a food delivery app that requires both restaurants and diners to use its service. Or even three, such as a consultant who receives their income from speaking engagements, educational partnerships and direct sales. Whoever your primary audience is, we will later be building your brand around *them*.

The big problem with our audiences, when it comes to communications, is that they are not us. We model our sense of what other people are like based on our understanding of ourselves, commonly overestimating the extent to which they share our beliefs. You know the phrase 'If you *assume*, you make an *ass* of *u* and *me*'? Well, it's true. They'll turn away if the message is not relevant and you'll miss your opportunity.

We assume many things when communicating with someone, including:

- What they know
- What they care about
- What motivates them
- How they behave
- Where they receive information from

As Dale Carnegie, the author of the classic book *How to Win Friends and Influence People,* says, you need to get them to 'see what you saw, hear what you heard, feel what you felt'. But other people have other dreams and fears. And they may respond to different triggers than you do. So unless you're talking to the mirror, you have to challenge your assumptions. Because you can only bridge people across to where you want them to be if you know where they are now.

Take the example of cycling. I might try to persuade you to cycle more by extolling its health benefits, because those are big motivators for me. I might relay facts on these benefits convinced this will lead to you ditching your car for short journeys. But this might not have any effect. For you, the main reason to switch might actually be that it could save you money on your commute, or that it would cut journey times. And I might have used those arguments on you instead, if only I had taken the time to get to know you better.

Let the profiling commence

Your primary audience might be quite broad. After all, 'customers' could be a huge ocean of humanity, with a few subgroups within it. When we look at these subgroups with a view to making the biggest impact, we might be drawn to the people that are currently furthest away from where we want them to be and focus our attention on them. Because, if we got *them* to act, that would be a *big* shift in behaviour. But, in fact, you should do the opposite.

First focus on those closest to you, those most aligned with your purpose (as well as having the biggest capacity and capability to act), as these will be the easiest to test ideas on and to influence. And once you have them on board, you will have an army of advocates who can actively support your message and do some of the work for you in terms of converting those harder to reach groups. (We'll return to this idea of engaging our advocates in the Active chapter.)

You can get to know your audience in detail by creating fictional profiles called '**personas**'. You might want to do this for a handful of profiles if you have identified a few subgroups. You can **download the audience profile tool** from the website (adamstones.co/influence) or just sketch it out. See the template on the next page – it's been completed with examples for one of the audience types for this book (I've added just a few points, rather than a robust analysis, to keep it legible). And please don't worry if you don't see yourself in this example – I have developed other personas!

Audience profile tool

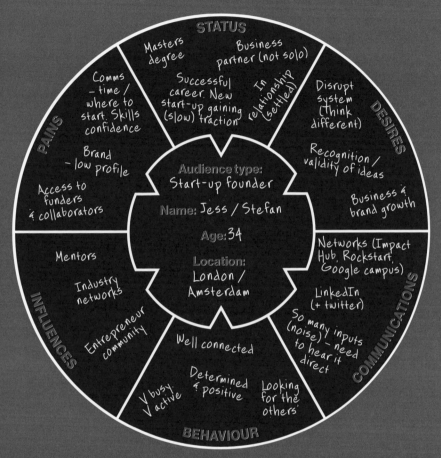

STATUS

Masters degree

Business partner (not solo)

Comms – time / where to start. Skills confidence

Successful career. New start-up gaining (slow) traction

In relationship (settled)

DESIRES

Disrupt system (Think different)

PAINS

Brand – low profile

Recognition / validity of ideas

Access to funders & collaborators

Business & brand growth

Audience type:
Start-up founder

Name: Jess / Stefan

Age: 34

Location: London / Amsterdam

Networks (Impact Hub, Rockstart, Google campus)

Mentors

LinkedIn (+ twitter)

Industry networks

So many inputs (noise) – need to hear it direct

INFLUENCES

Entrepreneur community

Well connected

COMMUNICATIONS

V busy. V active

Determined & Positive

Looking for the others'

BEHAVIOUR

THINK:
This book can help. It looks accessible, intelligent & practical.

FEEL:
It seems to understand me. I feel relieved. I feel empowered. I need it.

DO:
Buy the book. Share experience with peers. Share feedback.

BARRIERS:
Time / priorities – can I fit this in / is it important?

Author – who is Adam Stones?

Subject matter complexity – experience so far has put me off.

We use this tool to create a full picture, going beyond the usual demographics to tell the real story of the audiences' lives. This persona will then help you to later focus your communications to them, using some of the specific elements within it to inform everything from the type of words you use and your tone, to how you structure your offer, to the channels and tactics you use to reach them. It may also become a useful resource to refer to later when checking the validity of an idea or potential association, seeing how that connects with what the audience is really looking for.

So, let's dive in. First, after noting the audience type, give your persona a **name**, something you feel captures their personality (at least, as you imagine it). Then note their **age** and where they **live**. With these first bits of information, however generalised they are, you can really start to create a picture of someone who might typify this audience type.

Next, go deeper and capture information in the ring, from the following six headings:

Status: What is their professional life and educational background? What is their family situation?

Pains: What do they struggle with or worry about? What holds them back?

Desires: What do they want, need or hope for? What is important to them (their values)?

Behaviour: What does a typical day look like for them? How do they spend their free time?

Influences: Who do they listen to and turn to? What other brands or people do they like? What events do they attend?

Communications: What media do they consume? Which social channels do they use? How do they like to be communicated with?

To complete this comprehensively, it may take a little time. You should immerse yourself in their world, consume the content they do, listen in on the communities they inhabit, even go where they go. (Useful to note: by understanding their world, this process will also help you to identify more secondary audiences – and we'll come on to them in a second.)

Brand strategist Gareth Jones, founder of The Drawing Board, neatly describes the process I've just outlined as following three stages: Observe, Analyse and Empathise. He said: 'Once you've *observed* the audience from a variety of angles, to see the world they do, you *analyse* this information – what stands out and why? With this understanding, interrogate it with *empathy* to find the deeper truth behind what you've learned. You can then use this truth to guide your actions. As an influencer and leader of change, you should be selling the problem you solve, rather than the product you've created. That's why it's essential to really know what their pains and desires are – so that when you show them your idea, it makes sense, it connects and it gains traction in their world.'

So, what do you want them to do?

What is the point of an idea if no one does anything with it? Once the idea connects it must lead to an action. And to get people to change on the outside – whether that's to volunteer for your cause, buy your products or just improve the way they service your organisation – we must change them first on the inside. And to do that, we are not just talking about facts and figures but also – very importantly – emotions.

You know the old phrase, '**winning hearts and minds**'. It's *and* not *or*. We must stimulate both the left (logical) and right (emotional) sides of the brain. Think how many ideas have failed in recent years because they failed to bring out the emotional narrative (Brexit, I'm looking at you). When we connect emotion to ideas, they are more easily understood, more memorable, more inspirational. That's why we need to know the audience *fully*.

'PEOPLE WILL FORGET WHAT YOU SAID, PEOPLE WILL FORGET WHAT YOU DID, BUT PEOPLE WILL NEVER FORGET HOW YOU MADE THEM FEEL.'

– MAYA ANGELOU

To get people to *do different* – you have to first make them *think* and *feel* different. In *all* your communications, you are aiming for the following reactions from your audiences:

THINK – I fully understand what is being communicated and believe the message is important.

FEEL – I feel connected to the message, it has touched me emotionally and made me desire to be part of it.

DO – I am inspired by the message (and communicator) to now take action, to make a change.

We're now going to capture what we hope those changes will be for each audience. At the bottom of the tool first note what you want them to **do** (this could include categories such as purchase, protest, perform, pay, or perhaps even one that doesn't start with a p...). And within that heading, say a little more about what that change actually looks like in detail. Then work back and consider what you have to make them **think** and **feel** to get there.

THINK
I understand

FEEL
I am
motivated

DO
I will take
action

For example, let's say you sell shoes. You want your customer to buy the shoes, obviously, and then become brand advocates to their peers (*do*), so you have to make them *think* your brand has the appropriate cost, quality, style and production method, and *feel* that it will complement their lifestyle, connect with their values, and that by talking about you, they will be viewed more positively by others. That's a very simple take, but you get the idea. Capture your thoughts in the tool.

What's stopping them?

The next chapters will construct the identity, messages and tactics you'll use to guide the changes you want to take place. (For example, you want them to think you have an ethical supply chain? You'll need accreditation and stories of your production methods to share). But before we move on, let's consider what might stop your audience from acting. What are the barriers in their way? We need to understand these if we are to overcome them.

Let's stick with that cycling idea. Despite those great arguments we touched on, barriers for some people might be they feel a new bike will be too expensive, that the weather will stand in their way, that people 'like them' don't do that, that they love driving too much. Or they might feel they're not fit enough to even try. Well, there's a counter to all these ideas. And, whatever the push-back might be, we can categorise the barriers in three ways:

1. Belief: They hold negative *assumptions* about how something is or will play out.

2. Experience: Previous *experiences* indicate and identify barriers to them.

3. Passion: Their *values and passions* are associated with something they feel is in conflict.

Some of the barriers you identify may be easy to overcome. Just noting them will already help you to form a smarter, more inclusive and enabling approach to your communications. So, for now, list these potential barriers in the profile tool and note what's causing them. Later, we'll return to overcoming these challenges in much more detail.

//

CANVAS ACTION: You'll need the full audience profiles for other uses later (so be sure to complete them) but for the canvas just add in the types of your primary audiences and what you want them to think, feel and do. Of course, feel free to add more detail if you'd like.

//

Secondary audiences – stakeholders

Most instances of change are a collaborative effort. For ambitious change, this is absolutely essential. We can't do everything by ourselves but, by working with others who have compatible goals, we can aspire to something remarkable. This is not just about supporting you, but also about creating shared value.

For Business in the Community, a leading movement for better business in the UK, I worked with Forster Communications to help coordinate and launch a number of high-profile nationwide workplace mental health campaigns. With hard data and powerful personal stories, the *logical* and *emotional* case for each campaign was convincing. But we would never have reached the millions of people we did without close collaborations with the mental health charities Mind and Time to Change, as they gave the campaigns authenticity with both the media and the public.

When starting out with something, Psychologist Timothy Leary's well-worn phrase is useful to hold on to: **'find the others'**. Whenever you want to get an idea into the world, always identify who can bring that idea with you.

This mantra is something entrepreneur and consultant Paul Greenep testifies to. Paul is the founder of lifework, which builds resilience and responsibility into businesses. He said: 'When setting up an enterprise or just launching a new initiative, there will always be people who don't get it or say they don't support it. But if you only listen to them you may never achieve your ambitions. There will be other people out there that do get it, that will pick up and add to the idea, see something new in it and get passionate about it, whatever stage the idea has made it to. These are 'the others'. You need to know they exist as it helps you to keep going. Then you need to find them. They are out there!'

So, who will help make your ambitions become a reality?

Again, there will be many organisations or individuals that fall under this heading so we need to prioritise them according to how we will service our relationship with them. Let's use the 3 Cs to do this.

Step 1: Collate

First, list all the organisation types (or individual organisations or even individual people if that better serves your needs) that you will work with or alongside, who you can benefit from or who you need to keep close to. Look back at the list at the start of this chapter for some ideas for audience types.

Next to each name, you should note the role they will play in your ambitions. Two of the key roles will be to provide *access* or *influence*.

'Access' stakeholders open the door to a large cohort of your primary audience – or to further opportunities to activate your purpose – but might not necessarily be that influential. This could include a membership organisation with hundreds of members you'd like to get in front of, or a mission-aligned collaborator.

'Influence' stakeholders bring authority and relevance to your message because your primary audience already trusts them, engages with them and responds to them. This could be a trusted scientific body that will add credibility to your reports, or an individual 'influencer' supporting your products through their social media.

You don't have to use these terms specifically but do at least note why you think the names you list are important to you. This book, for example, could not have been made possible without *my* stakeholders: industry experts, publishers, designers and illustrators (all providing *access* to knowledge and skills), as well as community groups, membership bodies and professional associations (all providing *influence* through their support and endorsement).

Step 2: Categorise

The list you collate may be quite long so next divide it up according to how you will connect, using these three headings:

Listen – not working with them but you need to be aware of what they are doing and saying.
Inform – not requiring much interaction with them but they do need to be kept aware of your activity.
Engage – working with them in your plans or delivery, possibly as partners or collaborators.

For those in the **listen** group, you might not need a formal plan to do this, or you may set a regular schedule to check in on them or set a google news alert for related topics.

For **inform**, when you build your plan in the next step, be sure to include a reference to how you will actually keep (at least a few of) these informed.

For the **engage** types, you probably don't have the time and resources to service them all equally, and in fact you may decide to phase who you will engage with, according to the most urgent relationships. We'll also be detailing how our plans relate to this group later (which could include a network event for your partners or a mailer to your funders, for example). But for now...

Step 3: Chart

Let's further prioritise the engage group by zooming in on the ones that will be of most value to us. We do this by using the basic framework shown here, where on one scale we note their relevance to our ambitions and on the other, their effectiveness at performing the key role we have identified for them – i.e. their ability to provide *access* or *influence*.

Write all the names from your list down on individual post-its or pieces of paper and stick them on the wall or on your desk, according to this grid. Keep moving the names around until you have a manageable number in the top right-hand corner; the most relevant and with the highest levels of access or influence.

But even then, you may wish to focus further by considering the ease of engaging with them. When you actually begin to connect with these stakeholders, you're going to want to start with the easier names, as once you get a few of them on board, others will also be more attracted to your idea. High relevance means they may align on values and be likely to support you, whilst getting someone to speak on your behalf that is highly influential but a complete mismatch on purposeful relevance could fundamentally devalue your credibility.

///

CANVAS ACTION: List the key stakeholders that will support your efforts and note the role they will play. (Separately, keep a digital record or photo of how you mapped these stakeholders, so that you can refer back to it.)

///

HIGH RELEVANCE

LOW RELEVANCE

LOW ACCESS / INFLUENCE

HIGH ACCESS / INFLUENCE

Network network network

Building up your connections with all these audiences involves getting out there and identifying the opportunities to engage and impress. As well as physical, formal networks (which also might have great events to target for speaking opportunities), there are also virtual, informal networks (where people align around shared values or practices, often formed in social networks or online groups). You should look for opportunities in both types, identifying how to connect there with stakeholders (finding advocates, mentors, colleagues or collaborators), as well as with your primary audiences. Because, if you want to create change, communities that challenge and support you are essential.

Jon Woodroof runs Twotone, a brilliant cycling PR and sales agency. Building up his business from scratch, networking was crucial to getting established. And his key to networking success, he says, is kindness; doing things for people with nothing expected in return. He says: 'Try and find out how you can help the person you are speaking to. If you can do it on the spot, even better. By offering them value, you won't be forgotten in a hurry.'

SKILL BUILDER: As networking is an evolving skill right now, informed by the growth of online networks and conferences, you'll find this skill builder on the website, where it can be kept up to date. Check it out.

/PERSONAL SUMMARY

NEVER ASSUME: Try to appeal to everyone and you connect with no one. If you want to be personal, you need empathy. And for that, you really need to *know* your audiences.

PRIMARY V SECONDARY: Working towards your purpose will involve many groups of people. We split them into **primary audiences** (the main focuses of your change messages) and **secondary audiences** (organisations and individuals who support you and may also communicate with your primary audiences) – also referred to as **stakeholders**.

PROFILE PRIMARIES: We get to know the world of key primary audiences by three stages: Observe, Analyse, Empathise. To do this, we use the persona tool, mapping their **Pains, Desires, Status, Influences, Behaviours and Communications habits.**

THINK FEEL DO: Ultimately, we want these key audiences to *do* something so note it, along with what you need them to *think* and *feel* before they act.

BARRIERS: A number of factors may limit the audience's ability to act, based on their *Beliefs, Experiences and Passions*. You need to know these barriers if you want to overcome them.

MAP SECONDARIES: Change is a collaborative effort – map who you will work with or alongside. First *collate* the list, noting their roles (which may be to provide *access* to people or things, or to provide further *influence*). Then *categorise* (noting if you'll *listen* to them, *inform* them or *engage* with them). Then *chart* them according to their relevance and the impact of their role.

BUILD YOUR NETWORK: Find the others. Get out there and connect with people you can create shared value with. Always offer something helpful to be remembered favourably.

TINCT

We all have a brand. Every person, every organisation has a brand. But some of us are just not in control of it. **So let's take back control, because your brand is your secret superpower.** It's the core identity that will be brought to life in all your communications. **It's distinctly you.** It's like Superman wearing his underpants on the outside, kinda... **Now we know who your audience is and what you want them to do, here we follow the steps required to build and grow the brand you'll be taking to them.** From Vision and Mission to key messages, your Value Proposition and finding your focus for Thought Leadership (yes, that's you – a thought leader), this is Brand Boot Camp.

/WHAT IS A BRAND?

One of my early PR clients was a leading international branding agency. It was my job to tell the story of why they were the best, so I immersed myself in their work. As I did, I learned about the subtlety and power of brand development; how the right strapline can help you leapfrog your competitors, how a certain tone can create a strong emotional connection, and how some brands succeed in attracting attention by being bold and loud, while others rely on being calm and assured. Crucially, I discovered how all these things I saw on the outside were being driven by detailed, deeply strategic work on the inside.

And, of course, we need to apply the same rigour to our own brands. In this section, we will look at what brands actually are and how they are constructed, so you can build and live your own. You can follow this process to develop your personal brand or an organisational one – it works either way – but I recommend everyone starts by creating their personal brand first. Because, whilst 'branding' may seem to some people that are focused on positive impact as a 'nice to do' or further down the list, it is actually essential if you truly want to be successful.

I also suggest you start with your personal brand for the simple fact that you *already* have a brand. The work you do, the way you speak, the clothes you're wearing while you read this book... everything about the ways you think and act are connected with your personal brand. And all those things create a picture of you. But is it the picture you need if you are to change people's behaviours? Too often we allow this picture to be created by others because of our passive behaviour, rather than paint it for them with our active, conscious decisions.

Brands are more than shiny logos

When I ask people to tell me what they think a brand is, the common answers include 'a recognisable identity' or 'a clear offer', and there's some truth in that simple take. After all, the word itself derives from the brands left with branding irons on cattle and convicts, permanent markers of origin or behaviour. But if we spool back further to ye olde times, the word brand actually meant the fire itself, the source of that mark (and it still does in some languages). And that's what we're looking to create here; a blazing beacon of your purpose, to light your way and draw others to join you. This is what makes you *distinct*.

We mentioned **Patagonia** earlier as a 'purposeful brand'. It shows us what the future can look like and how its products and services will help get us there. When you buy a Patagonia jacket, you are recognising and investing in its purposeful philosophy, and you do so because of how that connects with your own values.

Another clothing retailer, **Nike**, is arguably one of the most recognisable brands in the world. It sells shoes, yes, but its *brand* is also built around an idea, theirs being a belief that any one of us can be an athlete or achieve great things. All we need to do, they say, is just lace up those sneakers. With its Colin Kaepernick-fronted ad campaign that includes the slogan 'Don't ask if your dreams are crazy. Ask if they're crazy enough', they tell the audience 'We understand you' and they make the audience feel both powerful and connected to power. And by associating itself with Kaepernick's values, Nike clearly signalled where it stood on a defining social issue.

Despite both brands taking different approaches and evolving in different ways, there are a number of things they have in common, and these are present in all strong brands, whether that's personal, corporate or non-profit:

- **A vision** of what the future looks like when they have achieved their ambitions.

- **A mission** that defines and guides how they will achieve this brighter future.
- **Values** that steer their *behaviour*, that are authentic and that we can connect with.
- **A story** of how they found their purpose and how they came to be.
- **A core offer** that is not about them but what they can do for us, to help us achieve *our* goals, *our* desires.
- **A style** of communicating – tonally and visually – that is recognisably theirs.
- **Clear positions** on the issues they care about and which give us opportunities for interaction, ensuring they are inclusive and alive rather than a passive logo.

These are the ingredients we will be building in your brand. Together, these ingredients create **Trust**, **Loyalty** and **Desire** amongst your audiences. Powerful brands create the environment around them which enables them to be a success.

'PRODUCTS ARE CREATED IN A FACTORY. BUT BRANDS ARE MADE IN THE MIND.' – WALTER LANDOR

Through all these brands, one thing that has given them longevity is consistency – we know what we will get. If Patagonia reneged on its values or if Nike products fell apart the moment you started running, all of the beliefs we hold about the brand would be taken away instantly. Trust, Loyalty and Desire would be destroyed. So they work tirelessly to shape and protect our perception of them, with products and services, experiences and marketing messages.

And whilst we might not have these big brand budgets as individuals, we must play the same game. Perhaps you're trying to use your business as a force for good (like Patagonia), build a tribe (like Nike) or trying to bring together the wide array of projects you have worked on under one, coherent identity (Unilever is a good example of this category). Something else? Whatever you want your brand to do, you will find examples you can deconstruct to help understand the ingredients.

If we were to similarly examine David Attenborough or Steve Jobs – people with strong individual identities – we'd see their brand success follows the same pattern; they tick off all these ingredients. They each have / had a promise of actions and a personality that is distinctly their own, as well as a consistent ability to uphold our perception of them. In fact Steve Jobs might actually be the definition of consistent style – look at any photo of him and chances are he's wearing white sneakers, blue jeans and a black sweatshirt. When he started telling us to 'Think different', his casual dress was a constant reminder of his creative difference to the suits of the sector we'd been used to.

The three Ps

You may have noticed three words come up regularly in how I describe brands. This is my definition:

PROMISE: At the heart of every brand is a promise: a commitment to provide specific products or services, underlined by clear values, consistency and competency.

PERSONALITY: Our promise is established, brought to life and communicated through our personality. The language we use, our visual style, the type of content we provide, the actions we take. These are recognisably 'ours'.

PERCEPTION: But, ultimately, a brand only exists in the perception held by the audience. Do they see our promise and personality the way we see them, or have we completely missed the target?

I break it down this way specifically to show you that no matter how you build your brand, you must understand the *perception* of it amongst your audience. We can say we offer intellectual value but if our audiences associate us with things that are dense and dull then that is exactly what our brand is.

Over the next two sections we will start to shape that perception by building your Brand Promise and Brand Personality using the ingredients we identified. Your brand is such an essential part of how you achieve influence, we're going to go into a bit of detail here. Ready?

a brand is the PERCEPTION

of a PROMISE

established by a PERSONALITY

/BRAND PROMISE

Successful brands are built by strategically mapping out a pathway to shape people's perceptions. When you're starting out, it can be enough to have an instinctive sense of how to do this but if we really aspire to influence, we need more structure and control.

First up is your Brand Promise, where we lay out what drives you, the future you are creating and the attractiveness of the approach you take. To build your brand, we'll dive deeper into that purpose you established earlier and, using what we now know of your audiences, produce the following core brand ingredients: **Vision, Mission, Values** and **Offer** (also known as your **Value Proposition**). And to do this, we'll also explore your **Uniqueness**.

It's worth noting here that *everyone* does branding differently. It's rare to find any two individuals or organisations that construct their brand in the same way – some have additional or fewer elements, some combine parts or swap the terminology around just to confuse you. So if you've seen branding broken down differently elsewhere, that's fine.

With the approach I lay out here, I've tried to create a framework that's simple enough for anyone to understand and apply but also layered enough to allow you to go deeper when, where and if needed. It's important you use this framework as a guide rather than a rulebook, because if you try to get it 'just right' you can get caught up in branding forever. So, to help synthesise all these branding ingredients, we will include one more element at the end of this chapter... **Why, How, What**. We'll use these three words to ensure you've covered everything you need to build a powerful brand *your* way. And I'll show how you can also use these words as the basis for a much more streamlined and rapid approach to brand development, for those that need it.

Vision and Mission

When it comes to understanding the difference between vision and mission, I love the simple metaphor shared by Anne Miltenburg in her book *Brand the Change* (an excellent resource for anyone wanting a really deep dive into organisational brand development). She suggests that *vision* is like the mountain peak you want to conquer, and *mission* is the steps that you'll take to reach that summit.

Of course, there are many ways to climb a mountain and there may be others approaching the same peak from different sides. Your mission captures the uniqueness and value of your way. Let's say you have a vision where malaria is wiped out. Your mission could cover scientific research, education, investment or technological advancement. It is worth noting the other paths that people will climb to the same destination – as it is likely that, at some point, you will help each other out. We talked earlier about 'finding the others' if you want to progress. That includes this group of people.

So, first paint a picture of your vision

When you picture the positive future you can contribute towards, what do you see? You will have already captured some of your thinking on this earlier so use that and expand on it to make it more clear. Sometimes having a strong picture of this vision – noting the detail of what's happening and who's there with you – can lead to new ideas for campaigns, products or partnerships, so go as deep and creative as you are willing to go. Your vision might not be something you stick on your website or talk about much, but it is crucial that you understand what it is: to lead a change, you have to be able to show people where you are taking them.

Here are some examples of visions:

World Health Organisation – *A world in which all peoples attain the highest possible level of health.*

Charity: Water – *A world where everyone has access to clean water.*

BYCS – *A future in which half of all city trips are by bicycle by 2030.*

IKEA – *A better everyday life for many people.*

Now, define the mission

What are you committing to in order to achieve this vision? Think again of Martin Luther King's 'I have a dream' speech. The dream of people not being judged by the colour of their skin was his *vision*, while his commitment to getting this idea into mainstream consciousness through such means as delivering that speech was his *mission*.

Some people use the words purpose and mission interchangeably, but that does both a disservice. Mission builds on and expands the drive you established in your purpose. Whilst a mission describes your path, your purpose captures why you are on that path. And whilst you can never wholly achieve your purpose, as it's what guides you every day, you can – at least in theory – achieve your mission.

To form your mission, take your purpose and turn it into a concrete, shareable statement – if possible, you want to outline what you are doing, who you are doing it for and why this is important. Your mission should be captured in a single sentence and be written in the present tense, with positive language. This statement will provide direction and motivation for your actions.

Here are some examples of missions:

Nike – *To bring inspiration and innovation to every athlete* in the world. *If you have a body, you are an athlete.*

Project Concern International – *Empower people to enhance health, end hunger and overcome hardship.*

PayPal – *To build the Web's most convenient, secure, cost-effective payment solution.*

Amnesty International – *To protect individuals wherever justice, fairness, freedom and truth are denied.*

As I said, don't worry about fulfilling some perfect expectation of what you need to capture here – everyone does it differently. Look again at Patagonia – its mission is bold in its simplicity: *We're in the business of saving our home planet.* Some missions are broad, some are focused. It's most important that it makes sense to you and is something you feel confident to share with others. And keep it quite top-level, like these examples, as we will go further into the detail of what you're actually offering in a minute.

//

CANVAS ACTION: Add your vision and mission statements to the canvas.

//

Values → Behaviours

Values are the essential qualities that sit within us, reflecting what is important. Therefore, we can use them to motivate and steer us, ultimately helping us to fulfil our mission. Moreover, clear values will ensure your brand and your communications activities are more consistent and authentic. Without values, we can lose our focus, lose our way and lose our audience's trust.

Perhaps a few words have already come to mind when you think of values: loyalty, creativity, collaboration, innovation, perseverance...

being a badass. Yes, these are all values. To find a collection that is authentically yours, consider:

- What qualities distinguish the way you think and behave?
- What words describe the way you want others to see you?
- What beliefs do you hold most passionately?

Of course, this might produce another long list. To streamline to just three to five values, ask yourself 'Can I really demonstrate that I live and work by this value?' Because they must be genuine.

Next, go further and – sorry, there's no other word for this – get more *value* from your values by making them more practical, **turning these passive values into active behaviours**. Let's say you value honesty. Might someone just say, 'Oh, you're honest. Great, because the other guy said he'd lie to us.' What does honesty mean to *you* – maybe it's being transparent on your research or sharing the ways you overcome personal challenges. Values should be understood and actionable, not vague and bullshitty. So you now need a short description for how you will use them to guide the way you behave.

For Metabolic, a global systems and sustainability company, we took the traditional value words and turned them into behaviours, phrased in a way that conveys the rebellious personality of the brand. Audiences are left in no doubt what they can expect if they work with or for the organisation.

Here is an example of a Metabolic value which others may have listed as 'boldness' or 'excellence':

Do epic shit – *The world needs big ideas and organisations who have the courage to follow through on making them a reality. Setting ambitious goals, engaging in pioneering projects and expecting a lot from ourselves defines who we are.*

You have to find ways to bring to life your brand values – steering daily behavioural habits – so your audiences know what you stand for.

CANVAS ACTION: Capture your values as behaviours in the canvas.

Uniqueness

We are all unique – our bodies consist of trillions of cells, our brains contain billions of neurons and we have millions of sensory experiences on a daily basis. There has never been and never will be anyone on earth... just... like... you. So why do so many of us try to act, look and feel the same way? You need to celebrate your uniqueness – you can use it help your offer stand out, to add credibility to a pitch and even as themes for great thought leadership content (all that to come...).

So we can draw on these qualities later, we first need to identify them. We're looking for around three to five statements here. We might call these your USPs, your Unique Selling Points. And as you capture them, consider what evidence you have for these claims and if there are people who can endorse these beliefs, such as on LinkedIn or your website.

Ask yourself...

Knowledge and experience: What have you learned or done that has given you the authority to be sharing your idea? So many of us sit on valuable insights that we forget others could benefit from.

Market differentiation: Look at where your audience is going for its needs – what's missing? How do you stand apart (be that simpler, better quality, more personal... whatever *the audience* needs)?

Vertical shift: Whilst many people look horizontally (expanding sectors in breadth with faster, better offers), how are you taking things in a totally new area, vertically?

Future-casting: You can't just be unique now but must also position yourself in the future, after all that's where the change will happen. So what trends are you spotting that you can help others to navigate?

And, what to leave out: You'll need to consider what aspects of your brand you focus on and what you need to keep as background noise. I came 3rd in the first-ever UK National Air Guitar Championships (purely for a magazine article, I promise...), but regrettably you won't find that top of my LinkedIn profile.

TO DO: Write down three to five USPs that complete the sentence, 'I offer unique value because...'

Messaging and value proposition

So far, we've got to know your brand better. We've even constructed some strong points to shout about. But our audience is still wondering, 'How do I fit into all this?' Here, we're going to look back on some of the notes you've made so far and use them to frame your promise in a way that leads to you becoming a magnet for the opportunities you deserve.

To do this, we'll complete a messaging framework

A messaging framework is a set of essential information that you can use to build different forms of external messages. Think of it as a Lego set of word blocks. (Who doesn't enjoy a little Lego building now and again?) And you can keep returning to the play set whenever you want, whether that's to outline your offer, tell your story, write the bio you need when you headline TED, or construct your rationale when applying for that big bag of grant cash.

In your framework, in its simplest form, you need to cover five main ingredients (or collect five different types of Lego blocks):

- **Who they are** (your audience)
- **What they want**
- **Who you are**
- **What you want**
- **What you offer**

As you can see, we have most of this already covered in your canvas. You have established their and your identities, as well as what they're looking for, what you want them to do, and the broad strokes of what you offer. But you need to go further with that last point. You haven't yet spelled out the fullness of the things that your audience can take from you or join you in (both physically and emotionally). You need to outline the products, services, communities and opportunities that you are offering.

Take some time now to really pull out what these are, nicely packaged as accessible and understandable vehicles of change. This might be the specific consulting services you offer, the type of consumer products in your range, or the ways that people can contribute to or get involved in your charitable work. (An example of how someone in the real world packages their offer is coming up shortly.)

When looking at what you offer, it's essential to weave in the relatable benefits of this to them; how you are turning their pains into gains, how you are turning their dreams into reality. For example, beyond bike nerds like me, most people don't buy bikes because they like collecting shiny geometric shapes with rotating parts. As we saw earlier, people buy them for their health, for getting to work or for just having fun. So consider what you are really offering – are you selling bikes or freedom? Selling your consultancy or how you make clients' lives easier, offering activism or change, a shoe or a lifestyle? You want to make clear the difference between their lives now, and their lives when they embrace your brand. Clearly capture the elements of this value.

Now use the framework to create a value proposition

With all the blocks in place, one of the most important outputs of your framework is a set of **value propositions**. We are trying to retell that value gain in catchy and connecting ways. Because once you can explain simply what you're trying to do, it will be much easier to get people involved.

I recommend developing **three value proposition types** here:

1. A strapline value proposition. This is sometimes called the *essence* of your brand, what really matters boiled down to just a few words. Think of it as your personal headline; grabbing attention and alluding to what else is to come, giving clarity and sparking curiosity.

2. A one to two sentence value proposition. Short and catchy. You can use this in bios, on website landing pages and short online profiles.

3. A one to two paragraph value proposition. This one gives more depth and understanding to your offer. You can use it to explain who you are on your website and as the basis for longer texts, LinkedIn profiles and funding applications.

And because it's easier to write something longer, you should start at the end and work backwards, creating a longer text and stripping it back in stages until you arrive at the strapline.

Let's see how this works in practice

Respected ecological engineer and Forbes 30 under 30 entrepreneur Dr Nadina Galle is someone who understands the value of personal branding. She has paid close attention to ensuring hers makes sense of – and demonstrates the value of – the various work streams she operates across. It's all based on detailed insights of who her audiences are.

She is on a **mission** to 'Build healthier urban ecosystems for future generations with emerging technologies'. (Note: she calls this approach 'The Internet of Nature', a brilliantly sticky idea.)

Her **strapline or essence** is: 'Make urban ecosystems flourish'. It's her brand in its purest form. (FYI my own strapline is 'Powerful communications, positive change', which is of course what led to the focus of this book.)

Building up, her **short value proposition** is: 'I inspire, inform and implement technologies to help urban ecologists and planners make decisions that pave the way for a greener urban future.' It's about her audiences, what they struggle with and what she can do, rooted in *their* needs, not a rallying call to join *her* mission.

Nadina breaks down her offer into three categories that unpack that proposition: *Inspirational keynotes, Informational workshops and Implementational partnerships.* Very neatly expressed and easy to understand, right? Within each category is a clear, value-led descriptor of what these mean and all together these form her **longer value proposition**.

If it looks simple, it's because she invests a lot of time in it. Nadina explained why: 'At first, I thought the value of branding was around elevating my profile and opening up new areas for my work. But now I understand it is much more powerful than that – it is about choosing the life you want to lead. It allows you to take control of your path and ownership of your freedom *because* of the greater opportunities it creates.'

//

CANVAS ACTION: Having identified what you are offering, write your strapline and short value proposition in the canvas. You won't have space for your longer value proposition here but include bullets for your offer if you can.

//

you
are the
GUIDE

your
audience
is the
HERO

Telling stories

From your messaging framework, another key output – or *construction*, to continue the Lego metaphor – is the story of how you will help your audience to realise their dreams.

In many stories, we meet a hero who is faced with a challenge and who then sets off on a quest. The hero is led or supported on this journey by a guide who understands what is required to overcome the challenge and who offers a better, alternative future. All the hero needs to do is act on the guide's advice. The hero's journey is both internal – a voyage of self-discovery – and external, a real physical act made possible by this internal change (i.e. because they've been led to *think* and *feel* different, they can now *do* different). At the end of this journey they must take that decisive action to overcome their challenges and to secure that better future. We see this story in countless books and films, from *Star Wars* to *The Lion King*.

Your brand can occupy this shape also. This construction also helps you to see with clarity something I first alluded to when revealing the *Five Traits of Influence*: you and your brand are not the hero of the story. As storytelling expert Nancy Duarte says, you are like Yoda, an authoritative and empathetic guide. Your audience is Luke Skywalker, the real hero, and you will help them by what you are offering, whether that's a new type of sustainable shoe, a social change community or even the secret to controlling objects and people across space with an invisible power called *the Force*. Ahem. Either way, your job is to lead your audience past their pains and towards their dreams, and your story explains how this will happen.

The five headings I mentioned earlier give you what you need to do this. But if you want to go a little deeper, I recommend checking out Donald Miller's StoryBrand framework. He takes the hero narrative I just outlined and splits it into seven distinct elements you can use to build a narrative for your brand. Check out his book *Building a*

StoryBrand for more detail on those steps and their practical application (especially as they relate to growing sales), or visit his site: mystorybrand.com.

Using your framework, your brand story might go a little like this...

Hello. I've noticed this challenge you're experiencing... By the way, let me introduce myself and tell you what gives me the right to be addressing this challenge... Now let me tell you how you can overcome it... Because, this is what you have to gain if you act, and this is what you can do right now to make it happen... And, believe me, you can do it. Are you with me?

Being able to tell this story is a helpful check that you have all the necessary messages captured in your framework. This narrative can be adjusted for a number of purposes, especially pitches. You can use it with this flow, or you can zoom in and tell a specific aspect of it. A key one is the story that explains how you developed your purpose (and how you came to be the guide), whether that grew over the years or in a spark that you can retell in a way that brings their senses to life. A strong brand is dependent on a strong narrative.

Mariah Mansvelt Beck is the co-founder of Yoni, the world's first brand of organic cotton tampons and pads to get on mainstream shelves. She told me that getting her story straight was a key part of forming powerful pitches when starting out. She said: 'I told my personal story. It was designed to immediately catch people's attention and it became one of the most valuable tools we had. And it worked – people had never heard of this idea before and some people hadn't even wanted to talk about it but, because of the story, people were suddenly connecting with the idea *emotionally*, and that meant they were passing it on.'

SKILL BUILDER: In the skills chapter we will dive into stories in detail: what makes a great story and how to tell them, for a number of purposes. So jump to page 158 if you want to know more.

Why How What

That may have felt like a lot of steps and a lot of detail. Believe me, as you grow you will come to appreciate all of them. Some aspects of your brand will live in the background, informing the decisions you take and how you express them, whilst some of them – like your value proposition – very much exist in plain view. But through all of these steps, we have tried to answer three absolute truths: why, how and what.

Many people try to jump in and show what they do without explaining how or why they do it, or they layer these on as afterthoughts. When they do this, they fail to get anyone to properly connect with them or their ideas, because they fail to show why they are valuable. That Simon Sinek quote again: 'People don't buy what you do, they buy why you do it.' That means we must *start* with why and make it the focus.

In Sinek's TED talk, he explains Apple's brand appeal. He surmises that if Apple started with the *what*, like many other brands, it might just say 'We make great quality computers. Buy them.' But it flips the order. And the narrative, to paraphrase Sinek, goes like this: 'We believe in thinking differently and challenging conventions (**why**), so we make things that are stylish and innovative to suit your lifestyle (**how**), and you'll see that in all these products – take a look (**what**).'

Because of this *why*, people connect better with the *whats*. You may be thinking, 'OK, that's cool, but it doesn't work for me.' It totally does. Let's see how those three aspects connect with the brand promise we've been building.

Why: The **purpose** that drives you and the **vision** you have for the world.

How: The **mission** you are on to fulfil this, which is guided by your **values** and **USPs**.

71

What: The **offer** you are making (products, services, experiences and campaigns within your mission).

So, instead of saying 'I am researching into material use in the built environment', try starting with 'I believe cities hold the key to leveraging a transition to a sustainable economy'. Instead of 'I make recycled drinking bottles', try 'I believe we must change habits if we are to end plastic pollution in our oceans' and note the difference in how people react.

You can use *Why How What* to check you have detailed all the information you need from this chapter. Or, if you want to start your brand lite and expand it later, just use these three words and the definitions above to guide your own initial brand promise – you can always return to this and build it up more robustly over time.

As I said, there's no 'getting it right' here, just getting it down, ensuring you have at least taken control. You might not come up with all the answers, at least not straight away, but the *process* of branding is so valuable. It forces you to really interrogate what you're putting out there. You have to make decisions that you might have been avoiding. And the result is a platform for a much more impactful application of the communications tactics and skills we're coming on to, knowing where you need to focus and what you need to filter out.

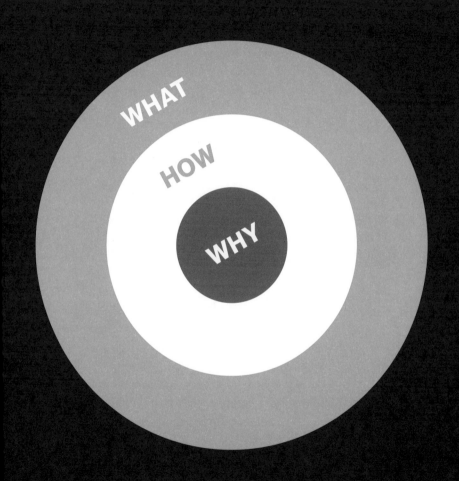

/BRAND PERSONALITY

Personality takes what is on the inside – the core promise – and brings it to the outside. If your promise guides what you say, then your personality guides how you say it. It's expressed in three main ways – the way you sound, the way you look and the way you behave.

By curating and cultivating your personality across these three areas, consistently, you build recognition, trust and favourability. Whether you're presenting on stage, writing a blog, sending a newsletter or updating your status, you should be recognisably *you*. And all those small points of activity build up to be something bigger than the sum of its parts, consistently helping people to understand what makes you special.

Of course, you already have a personality. This is not about creating something fake, but finding your authentic self and bringing it to life in a way that will connect. We all have our own natural style and it's important to embrace that. But we also need to be mindful of the ways we can strengthen areas, control others and grow in new directions – this is because we need to ensure that our communication not only complements our ideas but also marries up with what our audiences are looking for.

Capturing your personality

A useful way to capture the spirit of your personality is to explore the '12 Brand Archetypes'. Originally developed by psychologist Carl Jung, these capture and define the principal ways we humans approach life. We can use them to help us understand the type of personality our audience will best respond to and then use that to reveal how that personality would look, sound and behave.

Find your archetype

Take a look at the model on the next page. The central circle shows the four main desires we have for our lives. The next ring out goes a little deeper to show detailed expressions for these desires. In the third ring, you'll find the 12 archetypes that relate to those desires. These are: **Outlaw, Magician, Hero, Lover, Jester, Neighbour, Nurturer, Ruler, Creator, Innocent, Teacher and Explorer**. The final ring lists a couple of characteristics that are typical of each archetype.

Please don't feel overwhelmed if you're thinking 'what is this big spinny diagram thingy?' Some people will want to use it precisely to form a firm plan but for some of you it will just be a guide, helping you to ask the right questions in order to reveal more about yourself. Just give it a go.

Firstly focus on those two inner rings and consider which desires correspond with your audience's. What are they hoping for? Then work outwards to find the corresponding archetypes. With a number of desires identified, it's likely you'll land on more than one archetype. That's fine. Next, move out again to find the words that describe the character of the selected archetypes. This should be the personality your audience will best respond to. If you feel these words totally relate to your natural style too, great, you have a solid foundation to work from.

However, many people will find that what the audience is looking for and what you authentically offer don't fully align. You'll need to find some common ground. Perhaps you can find ways to adopt more of your audience's preferred characteristics whilst also making your natural archetype more appealing to their desires. Finding the right

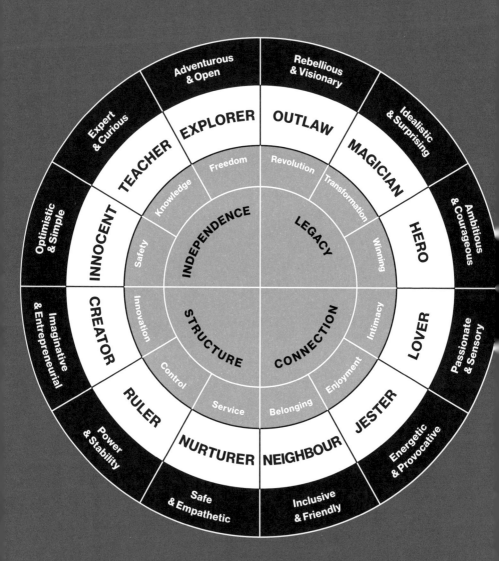

Teal areas: **Desires**

White areas: **Archetypes**

Black areas: **Character**

solution requires blending your strengths with areas of necessary development, so you can connect.

Once you've met in the middle, you'll probably still have more than one archetype. The end result is likely to be one type that is strongest and one or two others that you feel are also relevant but to a lesser extent. After all, even heroes can also be jesters, and vice versa. With your final archetypes, note the character words that are associated, and feel free to use the ones in the model just as a steer to create similar attributes you feel are more appropriate, if needed.

Your archetype and characteristics will help you to establish a consistent approach. For example, a rebel is more likely to launch a manifesto and host a flash mob, while a jester is more likely to use their wit to establish a bond, tell humorous stories and create playful video content. But, as with many aspects of communications, this model informs an art, not a science – you need to feel your way around this personality and make it your own. Just explore it and have some fun.

//

CANVAS ACTION: Capture your archetype(s) and characteristics in the canvas.

//

The way you sound (tone of voice)

We'll start to bring your archetype personality to life by first looking at the way you sound. Your expressions, vocabulary and emotion. Whether you're speaking or writing, we call the way you sound your 'tone of voice' and it should be consistent, wherever you appear.

Consider the playful tone of Innocent, a classic *jester* type – on their packaging they don't encourage you to call customer services but to chat to them on the 'banana phone'. Or look at Yoni, whose founder we met earlier. When it broke into the market to advocate for organic materials in feminine hygiene products, it matched its *outlaw* personality with a provocative tone in its highly effective slogan: 'Chemicals are not for pussies'.

Using the characteristics you have just established, unwrap each term to better understand how these might reveal principles you should apply to your tone. Let's say one of your characteristics is being 'straightforward', that might mean using clear language and being easy to understand. Or maybe you're 'friendly' – this could mean being inclusive, supportive and down to earth. Capture your ideas.

You can check out Mailchimp's Tone of Voice guide for inspiration here. It lays out the tone everyone in the organisation should take to be 'on brand' and you could write a similar summary for yourself. It goes: 'Using offbeat humour and a conversational voice, we play with language to bring joy... Whether people know what they need from us or don't know the first thing about marketing, every word we say informs and encourages. We impart our expertise with clarity, empathy, and wit.'

If you're not ready to write principles down now, at least spend some time to sit with your characteristics and ensure you are clear on how you could apply them, asking yourself where you sit on scales related to such things as **energy**, **formality**, **humour** and **empathy**. When you're more familiar with your brand, you can come back to this in more detail.

TO DO: Start to create a 'style guide' document for your brand (that we will add to later) by first noting your tone of voice.

The way you look (visual style)

Your visual style is more than what you wear (although that does create a strong first impression), you need to be aware of all the

ENERGY

FORMALITY

HUMOUR

EMPATHY

Choose your tone

touchpoints you have with your audience. Whether they watch your presentation, browse your website or grab your business card, they'll be getting visual clues to your personality. Here are some things you need to consider:

Colours: What is the main colour you will use, and which ones will be in the rest of your palette? Does your personality warrant bold neons or soft pastels?

Images: What type of photos will you use? Will they be lush landscapes or close-ups? Descriptive and capturing real people or abstract, conveying concepts? Professional or personal?

Illustrations: How will you bring ideas, charts, processes and statistics to life? Will your designs be clean or artistic, technical and detailed, or simple and attention-grabbing?

Icons: Will you be using these and, if so, how can you ensure they marry up with the rest of your visual style?

TO DO: Add to your style guide by capturing the essential visual traits that will be used to give your brand consistency.

The way you behave (actions you take)

The networks you engage in, the type of content you produce and the way you get your message across – essentially all the ways you interact with your audiences – will also be informed by your personality. Determining these actions will be a focus of the next chapter, but for now, it's important to pause and consider how your archetype might inform some of the ways you behave. Are you a protestor or a performer, a letter-writer or an occupier, do you document journeys or share discoveries? **Take a moment to think about how you will act.**

Identify focus of Thought Leadership

We'll round off our journey into being distinct by identifying the thematic focus you'll apply to what you say and do. Activating people to change will require you to share original ideas, outline unique points of view and reveal valuable insights. We call this 'thought leadership'; literally leading people's thinking by how you frame your own. It might sound like business jargon bullshit but, in reality, thought leadership is inseparable from *actual* leadership.

We need all your articulations of this thought leadership to connect, to add up over time, enabling you to become known for certain subjects that reflect your vision and mission. Therefore, you shouldn't engage in every subject of interest, but instead you should *focus*. To do this, we'll identify **three thought leadership pillars**.

Think of these pillars as forming the architectural structure that your individual bricks of messages will be built around. We pick three to ensure we have both scope (a diversity that reflects our expertise and how we fit into bigger systems) and focus (we cannot build our reputation if we spread ourselves too broadly). And we make them big, overarching pillars because we want our audience to think of us as being connected to big change, to think of us as being, well, a leader.

Depending on your brand, pillars could include the future of blockchain, racial equality, sustainable transport, reproductive rights, mental well-being... anything. Let's imagine you're trying to get your clothes rental start-up off the ground, you might pick pillars as: 1) Reinventing the fashion industry, 2) The circular economy, 3) Empowering individual expression. Whilst they might all seem diverse, they all add up, like a beautiful scientific equation, to form the sum of your brand essence.

Within these pillars, continuing this example, you might explore more detailed topics in your content on the environmental impact of fast fashion. Or call on more fashion brands to be transparent on their impact. Your Instagram page might share stories of people enjoying your brand, to show your big words are rooted in the real world... a diverse array, but all adding up to three pillars, supporting one fundamental idea – what you stand for.

So, how do you find your three pillars?

1. Purpose: Look again at your purpose diagram. The words you added for your skills, passions and what the world needs will naturally provide a wealth of authentic ideas.

2. Audience: What questions are the audience asking that others are not satisfactorily answering? You should explore things your audience both desire and need.

3. The others: Look at your peers, collaborators and competitors – what themes are they exploring that you could bring a fresh perspective to?

4. Uniqueness: Look at what you listed as your USPs – these can reveal passion subjects and experience.

Make a long list of potential focus areas and then streamline by testing their relevance and seeing where themes might be combined until you have three that together represent your essence.

//

CANVAS ACTION: Add your three thought leadership pillars to the canvas.

//

Turning pillars into content

One of the key expressions of your thought leadership will be in choosing a focus for the content you produce. Whether it's videos, blogs, talks, newsletters, guides, podcasts or infographics... content is all the *stuff* we fill our eyeballs and earholes with. And to get your brand out there, you're going to have to come to love producing this stuff.

You might categorise the thought leadership content you produce in four main ways:

- **Trends:** What's happening / is going to happen in a sector or system.
- **Opportunities:** An offer to improve the lives of your audience in some way.
- **Opinions:** Revealing a compelling case for a world view that underlines your mission.
- **How to:** Expressing expertise and sharing how others can understand and apply this.

And beyond the regular content types, there are also more valuable formats that require more time and effort. These include e-books, guides, digital tools and online magazines – it's stuff people bookmark, quote from and, most of all, shout about. This hard-working content can make you a destination, not just a voice. As you flesh out your plans in the next step, you'll need to consider what sort of content you'll be producing and in what ways you can stretch yourself to give the audience what they really want.

Brand Boot Camp. Done.

SKILL BUILDER: Learn how to turn thought leadership pillars into ideas for content and the steps needed to ensure this becomes *killer* content from page 144.

/DISTINCT SUMMARY

THE THREE Ps: A brand consists of three parts – a **promise** to provide certain products, services and campaigns (going deeper into the purpose you established earlier), and a **personality**, brought to life in the language you use, visual style and actions you take. But the brand really only exists in the audience's **perception** of you. Directing this perception is the key to an effective brand.

BRAND PROMISE: Your promise must cover three truths – **Why** (what's driving you), **How** (the way you go about things) and **What** (your offer to the audience). The elements within this we identify as:

- **Vision:** The peak of the mountain you are metaphorically aiming for.

- **Mission:** The steps you take to climb this mountain.

- **Values:** The qualities that steer you and are evidenced by your everyday **behaviours**.

- **USP:** Your unique knowledge, skills, experience and insight.

- **Value proposition:** The offer you are making to your audience to turn their pains into gains. This might be expressed as a punchy strapline (essence), a short descriptor or a longer overview. We can develop this through an adaptable messaging framework.

- **Your story:** You may use that framework to also develop a powerful narrative for who you are and what you offer. Or you might use it to zoom in and tell the story of how you found your purpose / became a guide.

BRAND PERSONALITY: If your promise guides what you say, your personality guides how you say it. To do this, find your brand archetype (one or more of 12 character types), with corresponding character-istics. And use this to develop:

- **The way you sound:** A focus for expressions, vocabulary and emotion – your tone of voice.

- **The way you look:** Approach to colours, imagery and iconography.

- **The way you act:** How you get your message across – more on this in the next chapter.

THOUGHT LEADERSHIP: A focused expression of your brand will be contained in three thought leadership pillars, all informing the ideas you share. These should add up to your essence.

TIVE

As we've established, you want your audience to think, feel and ultimately do something. That doing is what we are always working towards and that doing is what we mean by behaviour change. It may be getting people to buy a product, vote for a cause or switch habits. With any change, we are getting people out of their normal behaviours and leading them into new ones. In fact, leadership is really all about envisioning and enabling change. And to do that we can't just put our brand out there, cross our fingers and hope for the best. We have to get active. Here, we'll start by learning how change happens, then we'll form a plan to lead that change.

/CHANGING BEHAVIOUR

In 2011, a 16-year-old Dutch boy called Boyan Slat was diving on holiday in Greece when he realised he was seeing more plastic bags than fish. The idyllic ecosystems of his schoolbooks were in crisis and in that moment his life's mission was born. He had to do something to clean up the oceans. Everyone told him it was impossible, that his dream was way too big. But he kept asking 'why?' If the plastic wasn't there before, surely we can make it not there again. The following year, in a TED talk, he presented his idea for a machine that would collect plastic using the ocean's own currents to draw trash into a trap. His talk went viral and then, at just 18 years old, he founded the non-profit organisation – The Ocean Cleanup – that would build this first machine.

Today, thanks to investment from across the world, Boyan's team consists of more than 90 engineers, researchers and scientists. They have technologies gathering plastic at source – in highly polluted rivers – and in the ocean itself. If their current trajectory continues, they believe they could reduce the Great Pacific Garbage Patch by 50% by 2025 and are working towards a plastic-free Pacific Ocean by 2050. Considering the garbage patch covers an area three times the size of France, that's some mission. And all this started with an idea for change and the leadership to get on stage and talk about it.

Think like a system

The RSA (a brilliant social change charity I support) offers a useful philosophy that chimes with Boyan's approach and provides a lens for how we might all look at our change ambitions: 'Think like a system, act like an entrepreneur.' We might be working on a small idea but if we understand how we are contributing to the wider system – whether that's waste, transport, food, education, health or any other system – we will not only steer our way to making a bigger change but will also benefit from all the other changes and change agents in the system.

When Rosa Parks was arrested in 1955 for refusing to give up her seat on a bus that had enforced racial segregation, she contributed to the civil rights movement. We might call that a *shift in the civil rights system*. And it was the emphasis on how her idea was part of that system that made her action so effective. Always be mindful of the systems you are part of.

'THERE WILL ALWAYS BE PEOPLE SAYING THINGS CAN'T BE DONE. AND HISTORY SHOWS THAT TIME AND TIME AGAIN THINGS "COULDN'T BE DONE" AND THEY WERE DONE.'

– BOYAN SLAT

Shifting your audiences

Whatever *you* are trying to achieve, there is a single process you can apply to your part of the system. We might think of moving audiences along a scale, taking them from being totally unaware of our idea to eventually becoming vocal, placard-waving advocates for it. There are a few steps we need them to take to get there. And to articulate those steps I use the diagram on the next page, based on one developed by my friends at Forster Communications (the best in the biz when it comes to behaviour change communications).

As we go up the scale, we change emotions, beliefs and, of course, behaviours. As the audiences move from being *unaware* to becoming *advocates*, they also move from being *unfulfilled* to being *fulfilled*. And as this happens, your role moves from *informing* to *involving*; your approaches and messages become more personal and targeted (and, of course, the size of the audience decreases as not everyone will be moving up the scale). You need to understand where your audience is on this scale if you want to move them and even use them. You might need to tailor tactics for your ideas around specific steps on the scale, such as a campaign to raise awareness in a broad group or a newsletter produced just for advocates.

At each step, you also need to be mindful of the barriers that stand in the way of someone making further progress (you captured some of these barriers in your audience profiles) and what will help or motivate them to overcome these (more on this in the rules coming up). And you need to watch out for regression – the fact that people will sometimes slip back down the scale unless you recognise and reward their progress and offer repeated, refreshed, encouraging messages.

Of course, this is only effective if you have taken the time to get to know your audiences. As Peter Gilheany of Forster Communications says, 'At the heart of effective behaviour change is empathy. Too

Communications need to be repeated, reinforced and refreshed so you reduce regression and reinspire

UNAWARE	AWARE	DESIRE	ACTION	ADVOCATE
Status quo, stuck in habits	Understand but no connection	Feel change is needed & possible	Changing behaviour	Providing endorsement

Build understanding with broad, smart messages

Show you'll turn their pains / dreams into gains / reality

Outline simple, relevant beneficial actions to take

Make their experience positive & reward actions

Personal, tailored messages. Nurtured connection

often communication is about the communicator, broadcasting out an individual or organisation's thoughts, feelings and desires on a specific issue. The end result is just noise. Mould your communication around the audience's reality, not yours.'

The advocates you're looking to establish are what Seth Godin describes as 'your tribe'. In his appropriately-titled book *Tribes*, he says, **'A tribe is a group of people connected to one another, connected to a leader and connected to an idea.**' They are a powerful force – fighting for you, on your behalf, and massively amplifying your opportunity to be heard. One of your jobs as a leader is to identify, organise and activate this tribe, giving them the tools and opportunities to *advocate* your message to those that are still lingering in the early steps. We'll return to this idea shortly.

Sometimes, changing behaviour – even with your tribe behind you – can take a long time, and involve a number of interventions along the way. But sometimes – such as in a pitch to an investor or TED talk – you have to get people all the way from unaware to advocate within a few minutes.

Whatever your time scale, moving people along the change scale can be tricky. Changing behaviour means changing people and us people are fairly complex creatures. We don't always act in our best interests or even act on what facts tell us is best. We are often guided by ease, habits and emotions. Every time we're presented with information, we subject it to a range of interrogations, either consciously or subconsciously. We ask questions like *do I agree with the idea, do I understand it, how does this fit in with my existing habits and values*?

If we find ourselves asking lots of questions then we will just drop the idea. We have to just 'get it' and 'trust our gut' to get on board. That's because rational decision-making is taxing for the mind and we have evolved a series of mechanisms to avoid it altogether. Some of these subconscious elements include: confirmation bias (overvaluing information that confirms our existing beliefs), affinity bias (favouring ideas from people like ourselves), ambiguity bias (favouring known outcomes over risks), primacy bias (attaching more significance to information we see or hear first)... and there are many others.

But, if decision-making is strongly determined by such shortcuts, then instead of asking people to fight against their nature, we can capitalise on these factors and use them to our advantage. Whether you're launching a product, campaigning for change, encouraging a colleague or simply want to be a Jedi mind-master, there are certain rules you should apply to your change ideas and how you communicate them.

The 10 Golden Rules of Behaviour Change Communications

1. Clear

For ideas to spread they first have to stick. And to stick they must be simple to understand. Complexity can confuse and send people away. Remove any chance for ambiguity and interpretation. And speak to them in their language, not in your jargon. Even if the workings behind the idea are detailed and impressive, you must make it *appear* simple so people can grab hold of it. It needs to be so simple that you can explain it in one sentence.

Instead of using big concepts and big numbers to frame what you want people to do, turn these into visual images they can relate to. They need to *understand* before they can *act*. The book *Made to Stick* by Chip and Dan Heath gives the example of a non-profit public health group wanting people to adopt healthier diets. It discovered a typical bag of movie popcorn contains 37 grams of saturated fat. That's a huge amount but hard to comprehend, so the facts won't change habits on their own. So they explained, 'A medium-sized butter popcorn at a typical neighborhood movie theater contains more artery-clogging fat than a bacon-and-eggs breakfast, a Big Mac and fries for lunch, and a steak dinner with all the trimmings – COMBINED!' That got some attention.

2. Easy

Anything that might interfere with our routines or feel like a hassle can be quickly ignored. **Make changes seem manageable, not massive.** Make it safe to try, and easy to do – even if that means breaking things up and guiding people on steps towards a bigger goal. The more likely we believe something is possible, the more likely we are to attempt it. You don't start running by attempting a marathon on day one, you first set your sights on the end of the block.

One way to do this is to chain the desired new behaviour with an already-established one. So, if you want people to start a daily meditation practice, you might ask them to do it every night just before bed, rather than ask them to choose a random time each day. It's also important to make the desired change concrete. Instead of giving people the abstract goal of eating more healthily, we ask them to eat 'Five a Day' – the action is chained to already eating some fruit and veg, and provides a specific number to attain.

3. Positive

Concern alone doesn't lead to change. In fact, we often turn away from things that trigger a sense of anxiety or guilt. We react more positively to optimistic, gain-framed ideas. You can still be urgent, but reframe problems and challenges as solutions and opportunities. **The most powerful thing you can give someone to take action is hope.** People won't be inspired to act on climate if they think we're all screwed. But they will if you show that addressing it is possible and that there are steps *they* can take.

Being positive also means acknowledging loss. We have an inherent loss aversion, meaning we'll always consider what we lose out on by acting on one idea over another. So identify these losses and present alternative, more attractive gains. Don't focus on what you want them to *stop* doing but what they can *start* doing. You can also use their loss aversion to present them with what they will lose if they *ignore* your idea. Motivate them with both the gains of doing and the losses of not doing.

'FIGHT FOR THE THINGS YOU CARE ABOUT BUT DO IT IN A WAY THAT WILL LEAD OTHERS TO JOIN YOU.'

– RUTH BADER GINSBURG

4. Beneficial

People are unlikely to embrace something where the value is not clear. When you do show your audience what there is to gain, show how these benefits align with their lifestyles and values. Think broad here: consider the social, environmental and economic benefits. If the benefits are clear, then people may go further in pursuit of an idea.

Labelling, certification schemes or even network memberships can convey the positive impact of an otherwise intangible idea by giving an instant, credible impression of benefits. We all know the Fairtrade International label, for example – it provides clear principles and strict standards, which gives us *assurance* over the benefits of a product.

And the B Corporation certification provides proof of the good intentions of an organisation to operate for society and not just for profit. The techniques you use or communities you join will differ greatly according to the perceived doubt the audience may have (which may centre around financial, performance, physical, psychological or social concerns).

5. Relevant

Being relevant means understanding the various identities of your audiences and appealing to these directly. For example, they may care about climate but they may also be parents. You may get greater success by appealing to their desire to protect the future of their family rather than the future of coral reefs. Or you might get more athletes to eat less meat by appealing to their healthy lifestyles rather than their feelings on animal welfare. In this sense, relevance can be seen as being relatable: **help people to see themselves and situations they understand in the ideas presented**.

Often, understanding political leanings can help guide how you find the relevance. Social psychologist Robb Willer says that 'Liberals tend to endorse values like equality, fairness and care and protection. And conservatives tend to endorse values like loyalty, patriotism, respect for authority, and purity.' You could look at ways to frame your idea, using this insight. For example, Daryl Chen at TED.com says an appropriate climate message to conservatives might be to, 'Talk about how your country can show its leadership on the global stage by acting decisively to fight climate change. Or, how it could be a point of national pride that we preserve the beauty of our natural environment.'

6. New

We can't always come up with a totally new idea. But we can present it, visualise it and lead it in a new way. The photo entitled 'Earthrise' (a colour photo of the earth taken from space in 1968) showed our 4.5-billion-year-old home planet in a totally new way, exposing our vulnerability and union, and this helped people to connect with the idea of conservation more meaningfully, influencing new environmental movements. How can you show your audience's world in a new way?

Imagine if Mark Manson's phenomenally successful book *The Subtle Art of Not Giving a F*ck* was called something like *How to Manage Your Schedule*. Being new can involve being unexpected and surprising, to spark curiosity. **Get creative. Push boundaries. Create some friction.** This provokes people to think, which makes them much more likely to talk about it. You need to form a tribe around your idea if you want it to grow. And tribes simply don't form around boring, unoriginal, crappy ideas.

7. Normal

We humans are hardwired to adhere to norms. As Seth Godin says, our actions are hugely influenced by the question, **'Do people like me do things like this?'** We fear the unknown and so we unconsciously imitate the behaviours of those around us (especially those similar to us) – we call this social proof and it's why we're more likely to put solar panels on our roof if our neighbour has them. It can therefore be effective to target smaller – and often the most relevant – groups first. This sort of market segmentation allows control of communication, with time to react and adapt. Once we have shifted this group (up the scale in the earlier diagram), we use the social proof of this tribe to influence others into accepting something as normal for themselves.

And you must use the power of social networks – online and offline – to activate this tribe. When ideas are shared within networks, the social proof advocacy accelerates adoption. (This also underlines why social media influencers work.) The network then becomes a space in which your tribe can connect in a supportive community where action is welcomed and mirrored. Key point: once people love your ideas, make sure you nurture your connection with them and help them to share their love.

8. Rewarded

As we move people along our scale, we need to **keep rewarding them, to encourage progress and reduce regression**, whether that reward is financial, social or just a sense of pride. Frequent customers might get special discounts, people who sign up to your newsletter might get exclusive content or attending an event might offer a unique experience. Make sure you embed the idea of the reward into the perceived benefits of the action – dangle that carrot – as well as being responsively encouraging along the way.

If you have a language learning, meditation or exercise app you'll notice how this idea of rewards is built in to encourage regular use. They might show your 'run streak', telling you how many days in a row you have checked in, or offer virtual medals when you achieve a certain goal, or they might just send you positive messages about how awesome you are for being there. And we all like being told we're awesome.

9. Emotional

It is tempting – and perhaps easier – to focus on providing facts and information. But **a lot of decision-making happens on the right side of the brain, where we process feelings**. So we must create an emotional connection with the idea. That might involve humour or being personal in your approach, or connecting on a values level. Remember – people are interested in people so make sure you give of yourself.

And it will definitely involve telling engaging stories. Think about washing detergent adverts. They don't sell how clean the shirt will be (we assume it will do that) but show how that clean shirt makes you feel, especially when in the final shot our hero wears the shirt on a date with a person much more attractive than themselves. Stories help us to make sense of an idea and connect it to our world, and they are therefore a key requirement in our communications toolbox. (Read more on storytelling from page 158.)

10. VISIBLE

It can take several touchpoints before an idea sticks. It has to be out there, expressed through multiple channels, relayed by you and your advocates, and you need to keep repeating it. One blast on one channel by one person is never enough. When you develop a blog, you might explore how that can be recorded as a short video, expressed as an infographic, captured in a newsletter and cut up into chunks for multiple social posts. (More on this repurposing on page 154). How can you multiply your visibility while keeping your time investment low?

...and make it DESIRABLE

All these rules individually and collectively contribute to the essential goal of making your idea desirable. Have you heard the joke: 'How many entrepreneurs does it take to change a lightbulb?' The punchline is: 'It doesn't matter how many you have, you first have to make the lightbulb *want* to change.' OK, so I made that joke up and it's really bad. But hopefully it will be annoying enough to stick in your head and remind you that change doesn't happen by making people do things, but by making people *want* things. We need to *push* them out of their *inertia* by showing problems with the current situation and *pull* them past their *anxiety* of change by showing the benefits of the new idea.

Look at how cities adapted to Covid and started to prioritise access for walking and cycling to enable people to get about and maintain healthy lifestyles. Whilst many people said, 'Finally, some progress', there were also voices of protest. Despite the quadrillion benefits that active streets bring to health, the environment, safety, local economies and accessibility (to name a few), there are still people fighting it. Why? Because people are creatures of habit, they do not like being told what to do and they won't necessarily act in their own interests unless you help them along the way.

Before you start trying to get any idea out there, you must always consider what the pushback will be. Remember, often objections do not come from a position of *hate* for your idea but from a position of *love* for something else. You have to find out what that passion is and use it, connect to it. A protestor from the above example might simply be mourning the idea of *any* change to their community. This might indicate they also mourn the loss of traditional community values. So you could show them how the new idea actually helps to *restore* community connections.

To ensure they land, the rules above should not only be targeted but also used in combination: strategies that influence understanding and adoption of ideas must be combined with those that enable and embed new behaviours, and you must combine high feasibility with high impact. **Next time you are moved by something, see how many of the rules have been applied.**

PUSH PULL INERTIA ANXIETY

/ACTIVE SUMMARY 1: CHANGE

THINK LIKE A SYSTEM: When planning your ideas and actions, always consider your place within the system, to identify ways to make a bigger impact and meaningful connections.

SHIFT PEOPLE ALONG THE SCALE: Change can take time. You need to move people from being unaware to being active and then advocates by understanding their barriers and motivations, and by targeted interventions at every step.

ACTIVATE YOUR TRIBE: Your advocates are bonded to you, your idea and each other, forming a tribe that's fighting for your idea to succeed. Identify, celebrate and motivate this tribe always.

USE THE TEN GOLDEN RULES: Our decisions are largely based on subconscious decisions. Influence these by making your ideas...

1. CLEAR: Complex ideas confuse and scare. To make yours stick they must be simple to understand, with clear language and visual imagery.

2. EASY: Make ideas manageable, safe to try and easy to do – never a hassle. Try chaining the desired new behaviour with an already-established one.

3. POSITIVE: The most powerful motivator for action is hope. We turn away from anxiety and guilt but tune in to optimistic ideas.

4. BENEFICIAL: Show your audience what they gain and make these benefits align with their lifestyles and values.

5. RELEVANT: Help them see themselves and situations they relate to in the idea. And make it timely; connected to what's happening in the whole world and their world.

6. NEW: Be surprising to spark curiosity. Get creative. Be bold. Create friction. We can't always have totally new ideas, but we can make them feel new.

7. NORMAL: The big question we ask is 'Do people like me do things like this?' – show them that they do by activating your tribe of advocates.

8. REWARDED: No one likes to have their hard work go unrecognised. As people move along your scale, reward them, whether that's financial, social or just a sense of pride.

9. EMOTIONAL: A lot of decision-making is led by emotions, not reason. So connect on this level and use stories to convey these emotions.

10. VISIBLE: It can take several touch points before an idea sticks. Repeat and repurpose your messages in multiple ways on multiple channels, yourself and through your stakeholders and tribe.

/PLAN OF ACTION

It's time to use all the insights you've gathered in this book so far and turn your ambitions into a strategic plan that you can measure the success of. Given that every reader will require different levels of detail to their plans – depending on where you are right now with your communications journey – I have created a versatile template that aims to be relevant to *every* reader. But before we get into that, let's first get to know some of the touchpoints you'll be using in this plan.

Your channels

Think about where you get your information from – newsletters, blogs, LinkedIn articles, that guy by the bins by the supermarket (just me?). We refer to all these sources of information as channels. In your audience profiles you will have already captured a few of the ones you need to hit. And no doubt you're already using a few. But let's just run through the main channels available and consider how and when you might want to get them working.

To do that, we'll use the PESO model. This might sound just a little jargony but it's a simple way to help us categorise and prioritise these channels. It stands for **Paid – Earned – Shared – Owned**. But as you'll see on the next page, I like to flip it and call it the OSEP model – because that's a more useful way of showing how we step our way through it and, well, because I'm like that.

OWNED	SHARED	EARNED	PAID
Things in your control	*Things co-owned or contributed to*	*Things secured through relationships or influence*	*Things you pay for*
Your website: Stand out above those who just have social profiles. An interactive showcase for your brand. **Your events:** Any event / experience you organise. **Your emails:** Newsletters or other email communications. **Your content:** Not a channel but still owned; podcasts, videos, articles – it builds the brand, and services your audience's needs.	**Social media:** We 'own' our social channels and put our owned content there, but they are in a shared network, a result of interactions with others. **Other events / networks:** Any events or conferences you attend or networks you play a role in.	**Media, bloggers, influencers:** Gain attention by sending out press releases, conducting interviews, performing publicity stunts. **Third-party sites:** Securing spots for your content on other websites and digital platforms. **Stakeholder channels:** Doing the same but for channels managed by a stakeholder, i.e. their newsletter. **Speaker platforms:** Getting on stage at events and conferences.	**Social ads:** Adverts on social media, usually containing a visual & short message. **Search ads:** Ads or priority listing on search engines, usually containing a short message. **Sponsored:** Paying to place content (such as a blog) in influential channels or paying for gains, such as sponsoring an event to secure a speaker slot or having an influencer promote you.

Using the OSEP model

Traditionally, we start focusing on the owned channels and work to the paid ones because it is cheaper, easier to control and, of course, there is no point spending money on ads if they're driving people to a shitty website. But that's not always the case and each step has its own considerations...

OWNED: You should always make sure you are *owning* your *owned* opportunities, even if that just means having a strong online profile. This could be your LinkedIn page or a personal website. Don't think of this as just a shop window but more as a welcoming experience centre, where people can interact. All the other channels will be signposting people back to these in some way, so make sure they're bringing your brand and ideas to life, with a clear value proposition and call to action, along with case studies and testimonials showing your credentials. And ensure they're kept fresh with good content for the audience to digest. Your online profile will be many people's first impression of you so don't let it be their last impression also.

SHARED: Many of you will be building a presence – or even community – on social media. If that's where your audience is, it makes sense to go there too – putting yourself into conversations that could potentially be seen by millions. But getting it right requires some strategic thinking, with millions of people vying for the same eyeballs. And once you've mastered the latest TikTok, there's always another Clubhouse just around the corner. So, don't spread yourself too thin. Wherever you are, you should be committed; alive and active, regularly and visibly sharing useful ideas.

EARNED: These channels can require more time (especially building up the valuable relationships you need to pitch your content to) and skill (such as producing a level of content that others will *actually* want to publish) – and we will learn about building these relationships and skills in the next chapter. But when you *earn* visibility, the value of the profile it gives you can be enormous. People will place fundamentally more importance on someone else telling them your ideas are awesome, compared with just hearing it from you.

PAID: Getting to paid last is not a strict rule. It may be hard to drum up attention to promote an upcoming event related to your idea, for example, if there is no 'news value' or your social following is small. So you might jump straight to some targeted LinkedIn advertising, getting your event sign-up link in front of the niche, hard-to-reach audience you're after. And you can start small, to try it out, giving your site or post a targeted boost for relatively little investment.

As the book *Traction* by Gabriel Weinberg and Justin Mares explains, **there are so many potential channels available to you, you can never operate across all of them in any effective way**. Nor should you feel you have to be present on a certain channel just because it's new and shiny. For some people, a weekly newsletter might build your community better than Instagram stories. For others, the opposite. Each channel will have essential functions related to your needs, whether that's community building, campaigning, fundraising, sales or brand awareness.

To gain traction in your channels (i.e. to get them serving their functions), you should start with what's possible – identify a long list of OSEP channels you think could serve you. We'll call this list your *channel map* – it should be based on where your audience is active or where you feel untapped potential exists. Then, once you've activated these channels, keep checking their effectiveness to see what's working. With this knowledge, refine the map down and focus your attention on the most effective channels – these will become the engine room of your day-to-day communications.

Once you have your channel map, you also need to identify what you need to do to make these channels fit for purpose. This might include: buy a domain and build a website, update your LinkedIn pro-file with your new brand messages, list networks to join, commission photography for your profile or capture media targets for your PR campaigns. And we'll go into how to carry out some of these examples later. Ensure that wherever people come into contact with you, you create a consistent and effective *perception*. (Quick note: If you want to dive deeper into your communications plan first, read on and come back to your channel map later.)

///

CANVAS ACTION: Note the channels you will use on a regular basis and their main functions in the canvas and, separately, note the actions required to get these channels up and running.

///

SKILL BUILDER: Head to my website for some pointers on rising above the social media noise to get the attention and traction you need.

Create your comms plan

OK, now let's set up that plan. The process I outline here has five steps. There are other ways to create a plan that are more complex and comprehensive, but this is pretty compact. And it's therefore versatile – you can fill it all in with mind-blowing, technicolour detail to create a robust approach or just make notes in the bits you want to focus on to give you a starting steer. Whatever *your* needs, we'll walk through it together just the same. And later, I'll outline how to simplify things further, if you need to.

Objectives → Actions → Outcomes → Commitments → Support

Take a look at the example comms plan on page 113. It contains examples noted down by Tom, a made-up person who's going to help us see how one person might use all the steps. Tom is a young entrepreneur who's been supporting people experiencing food poverty in his city. Based on this work, he's now setting his sights on his vision to tackle food poverty in cities across his country. So, he's on a mission to build his fledgling community of volunteers and activists (to share ideas, collaborate on campaigns and provide peer-based learning opportunities). And that's why he picked up *Influence*. Read through the guiding notes that follow and see how Tom addresses each step. As you can see, he's got his work cut out to realise his dreams. But this plan will help steer his success. (This is not the whole of Tom's plan as the list would be too long for the page, but it gives you the picture.)

Download your own template plan from my website or sketch a copy. Later, we'll be transferring some of the main points to your canvas.

Step 1. Objectives / Summary

Set your ambition for the year ahead
Before we list specific tactics, what will this activity be heading towards? You have your mission but that's too big. We need to take steps to get there. For some people it can help to set SMART objectives here: plans that are Specific, Measurable, Achievable, Relevant and Time-bound; clearly defined, with a deadline for achieving them. Most experts will tell you 'make all your plans SMART' so you have a very clear, accountable focus.

But I appreciate that some of you are simply not ready to do that, and perhaps you're not looking for a full-on strategic plan right now.

So, you can also just provide a summary here, a sort of bird's-eye view of where you're going or how communications will support your bigger goals, so at least you can see you are progressing with purpose. It might just be the shape and scale of all the activities you'll be undertaking that involve communications.

As you can see in the example, Tom captures his objectives more simply, as three overarching ambitions. You could choose to be even more narrative, or more SMART and detailed. And also note: if you already have business or organisational objectives captured somewhere, ensure your communications objectives complement those.

Step 2. Actions

Turn what you want to achieve into how you're going to do it
Take a look at all those 'do' actions you listed for your primary audiences, and all the functions of your key stakeholders – what action do *you* need to take, to get them to perform *theirs*? You want people to buy something? You have to get the sales opportunity right in front of them, get influencers and advocates on board, and create a website. You want people to invest? You need to pitch, establish your thought leadership profile and build your network. You want to grow a community around an idea? You'll need community stories, digital experiences, events, and maybe a TED talk.

Like Tom has, you can identify some tactics by looking at the channels in your mix and brainstorming ideas around each one. So, maybe Instagram is important for you – how will you activate this? But be mindful of what is achievable. For podcasting, for example, it can take time to build an audience and doing so will require a certain consistency of output. Can you commit to that now? Instead, you might first look at where you will make quicker gains, getting yourself into other (already successful) podcasts as a guest, or get comments in the media, or place your thought leadership pieces where your audiences already hang out.

Step 3. Outcomes

How do you know your actions are working?
The next step is to note what outcomes you'd see as ideal measures of success; the indicators that you are working towards your objectives. For some people this may be ambitious, like a certain number of national media mentions, a number of sales, or the size of their community. While for some of you it may be more simple right now – a promotion in your workplace or landing your first public speaking gig. Note the shifts you want to see. Capturing these gives you something to check progress against. (And we will return to them later when we look at how to evaluate the impact of your approach.)

Step 4: Commitments

The time and effort you'll need to put in
Whatever you listed as your actions earlier, it's likely they will fall into two types: **ongoing** and **focused.** The former is what you do every week, the cycle of activity that keeps your brand out there, such as maintaining social media communities or sending a regular newsletter. The latter – which we might call *spikes of activity* – will be carried out over a defined period of time, with a very specific ambition in mind. These might include launching an annual report or seasonal customer drive, for example.

Ongoing communications

Across ongoing comms, step 4 is to capture the commitments you need to make in two main ways: the **rhythm** you can stick to and **outputs** targets to hit.

Rhythm: Try and set a rhythm for your communications, such as an hour a day or two hours a week. How much time can you realistically commit? Then divide that into how you will assign that time, such as splitting it between social media, content generation and network building. You will be a much more effective communicator if you have a regular rhythm helping you work towards your goals, rather than thinking, 'I've got a bit of time today – er, what shall I do?'

Outputs: What are the *outputs* you need in order to generate those success outcomes? As Tom plans to raise his profile as a thought leader, he commits to producing one quality article per month. You'll need a certain level of output to hit your ambitions.

Focused communications (spikes)

You should map your spikes in your calendar to ensure you know what's coming up and how this relates to what's happening in the world. It can also help to have a separate comms plan specifically for each spike. This doesn't have to be complex but clearly Tom's plan for a research report, for example, will need a little detail behind how it will be communicated. You can either use the same five headings as the general plan or use a more detailed plan (and you can download a template for this from my website if it helps). Every spike will have different requirements in terms of the time and effort you need to put in. They may have different audience focuses, different partners involved and very different content and channel uses. So, using this tool will help to clarify exactly how you're going to make it work.

Step 5. Support

What skills, assistance and resources are required?
The final step is to detail the support you'll need for all this to happen. It can be a long process to get all the pieces in place, and plotting them makes planning a whole lot easier. Here's some more information on each category:

- **Skills:** Looking across the skills detailed in the next chapter, which will you need to focus on for your actions to be successful? List

COMMUNICATIONS ACTION PLAN

OBJECTIVES / SUMMARY

1. Grow community impact – communicate the activity & potential of the community to grow size and effectiveness. 2. Build profile – of my brand & the community impact – to raise community profile. 3. Attract partners and funders to support us through targeted comms.

Actions	Outcomes	Commitments	Support
Partner with research body to identify scale of food poverty. Use this for major report. Target media. Publish thought leadership articles on food poverty scale and solutions. Speak on this at conferences / events. Organise online summit for community with wider stakeholders. Use this to launch monthly newsletter. Build Instagram community with stories of volunteers.	Spoken at 5 events. Newsletter grows to 20,000 subscribers. Website visits doubled, social media connections and engagement up 30%. Mentioned in 5 x national media outlets. Volunteer network reaches 500 members. 1 headline funder and 5 small funders confirmed.	Rhythm: (10 hours per week + 1 spike per six months.) • Social media: 40 minutes each day engaging • Content: 2 hours per week on writing / production • Skills: 1 hour per week on developing • Network: 1 hour per week on connecting and sharing ideas across my networks Outputs: • Write 1 x article per month • Connect with 2 x journalists per month • Pitch to 2 x events per month	Skills (inc. scores): • Conversations 5/8 • Storytelling 4/8 • Writing 7/9 • Public speaking 6/9 Assistance: • Outsource PR (if funder on board) • Web developer • Graphic design volunteer Resources: • Website improved • New community newsletter • Strong speaker bio to pitch

all these skills, and next to them give two scores. Firstly rate your current competence (score out of ten) and secondly set a bold ambition for what you'd like your score to be in a year's time. (The next chapter aims to help you bridge that gap.)

- **Support:** You may need additional professional skills not listed in this book (such as filmmaking, photography or website development). You may require extra brains and muscles to help work through crunch periods or ambitious plans, or perhaps online tools for things like graphic design.

- **Resources:** This category is all the things people see and touch in connection with the actions. It may be an annual report on your impact to support a pitch to funders, an online tool to help your community carry out an action, or even a campaign web page to ensure people know how to get involved. This stuff can require a lot of preparation.

Simplify to suit your needs

For some of you, where planning is not as important as creating a brand or building skills right now, a simpler approach may serve your needs perfectly well. This could include knowing the essential focus of your plan (a summary of your ambitions), along with mapping your main channels, and detailing the frequency and ways in which you will serve these channels. This idea of being strategic but flexible is supported by Jennifer Mulder, a respected psychologist and the founder of The Health Sessions, which provides advice to people with chronic ill health. She told me that the way she adapts her communications plans to account for her own health challenges can be a lesson for *anyone* concerned about getting their planning 'perfect'; that a 'lite' plan can still be the 'right' plan.

She said, 'SMART objectives can definitely be a helpful and effective strategy. But as we've seen a lot recently, many things in life can get in the way of our best intentions. This is something

I've experienced for years and so I know how easy it is to feel a failure if you miss your targets. So, I now focus on the *direction* of my goals and a doable daily rhythm based on my circumstances rather than beat myself up about how *specific* or *time-bound* I am being. This is allowing me to adapt and enjoy the steps along the way, helping me to achieve my dreams whilst being realistic about how unpredictable life can be.'

//

CANVAS ACTION: With your plan completed to the level of detail you require, transfer the objectives – if you have them – into the canvas, along with a summary of the actions you will take. Also list the overview of your commitments. And in the next canvas section – 'Skilled' – add in the skills you need to focus on, along with the scores you noted.

//

Evaluating your success

The Sheila McKechnie Foundation is a brilliant UK organisation working to unleash the power of civil society. As CEO Sue Tibballs says, continued adjustment to how you are *active* is essential if you want to create impact. She said, 'Change is complex. It requires constant review of strategy and tactics, repeated checks on values and ethics. It necessitates endlessly scanning the state of the world to ask "where does power lie now?", "what trends are affecting the change we are seeking?", and "who can we get to help?"'

An effective communicator is always sensing and responding to the messages coming back. It's important to learn from your activities, to ensure you can refine your approach and become more impactful. You can do this in two main ways: a large scale review every six months or year, and a more simple check-in every month.

The big one

Knowing how many Instagram followers you have or how many people share your content is not enough. You also need to know what *impact* this reach and engagement is having. Having a tangible measure of this will mean you're better prepared to convince others of your promise, to wow funders or recruit great collaborators.

You can use this simple grid to audit your success. First, plot the outcomes (success measures) you developed in your comms plan. Then in the following columns note what was actually achieved and what impact that led to. Finally, note what lessons you can apply.

IMPACT AUDIT			
Outcomes (success measures) planned	**Outcomes (success measures) achieved**	**Impact achieved**	**Learnings**
What were the success identifiers you listed in your comms plan?	*What were the actual results?*	*What changed / what actions were taken / how did you progress your mission?*	*What have you learned that you can use to adapt your strategy?*

You might find a particular channel is underperforming and can be dropped. You might realise a stakeholder is providing great access and needs to be nurtured, that a message isn't sticking as you'd anticipated, or that a tactic has totally flopped. You may also discover your brand perception is off the mark or that you need to work harder at developing your skills. Use this grid to celebrate achievements and identify focuses for growth. (Of course, you can also use this evaluation model after every spike too, if they are significant enough.) Based on your learnings, you can update your comms plan or your entire canvas.

'THE GREATEST TEACHER, FAILURE IS.'
– YODA, *STAR WARS: EPISODE VIII*

The regular one

I also recommend a quick weekly or monthly check-in, to gauge how you're doing and see if any simple refinements can be made. One of the most simple and effective ways I've discovered to do this is called **Plus Minus Next** (developed by Anne-Laure Le Cunff of Ness Labs). With just three columns in a notepad or a doc, it works like this:

- + **Plus: What's going well?** List all the things that are progressing. Celebrate them and draw motivation from them.
- - **Minus: What's not going so well?** List where you're falling short, without blame, and reflect on why this is.
- > **Next: What will I do about that?** Note what you're going to change as a result of these insights and set a clear marker for progress that you can check in on next time.

So simple. You can also use this handy technique after individual comms actions, such as a speaking gig or when you post an article. How was it, what's one positive and one area to improve?

Before you put the lessons of this book into action, do a stocktake of the size and engagement levels of your audiences in various channels so you have a benchmark to measure success and impact against.

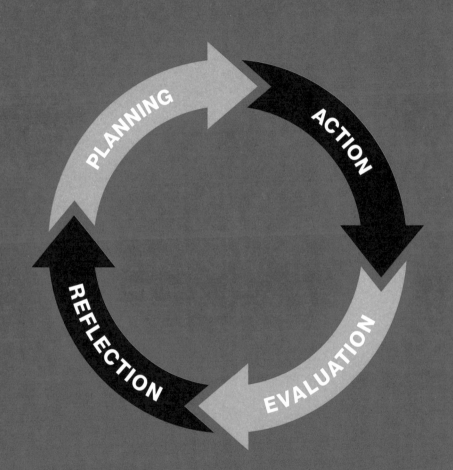

/ACTIVE SUMMARY 2: PLANS

MAP & ACTIVATE CHANNELS: Map where you will be active across the OSEP channels (Owned, Shared, Earned, Paid). Find your focus (the channels your audience use and that provide the greatest opportunities for impact), list their primary functions, and make sure they're fit for purpose. #1 rule: own your owned channels with a clear and consistent online presence that shows off your promise and personality, and offers ways to engage with you.

ACTION PLAN: Follow the five steps: First turn your ambitions into **objectives**. This could be SMART or a summarising direction of travel. Then assign practical **actions** that will make that happen (based on what you want people to *do* and your new understanding of how change works). Then identify what successful **outcomes** for those actions look like (either measurable results of success or indications of shifts in behaviour). Next, list the **commitments** needed (the time and volume of work) across ongoing and focused spikes of communications activity. Finally, list the **support** needed; all the skills, assistance and resources required to make your ambitions a reality.

SIMPLIFY TO SUIT: It's good to set a bold ambition. But also be mindful of the effort required. Ensure you at least have a clear ambition if SMART objectives are too much or not needed right now.

EVALUATE SUCCESS: What effect are your plans having? Perform an impact audit at least once a year and use the resulting insights to refine your plan or even your canvas. Also check in once a month on progress with the Plus, Minus, Next model. Then give yourself a high five.

LLED

You have your assignment. You've got your superhero outfit on. Now let's hit you up with the gadgets... **If you've flicked forward to this skills chapter looking for a quick boost before a big talk or article deadline, then go ahead, dive in.** But you will really only get the value needed from this chapter if you have already worked through the rest of the book. **Because if you want to build skyscrapers – not sandcastles – you need the best foundations.** The skills selected for this chapter are the core essentials, enabling you to deliver your messages to any audience, in any place. **Let's do it.**

/BODY
LANGUAGE

When we speak, our wonderful, wobbly bodies offer visual clues as to who we are and what is truly being said. In fact, research suggests that more than half of the meaning of what we say is conveyed by our bodies. These movements are interpreted by the listener instantly, deep in the brain, in an area that has been processing information since before humans could walk or talk. So if we want to be understood and make a connection, whether that's on stage or in person, we have to first understand this ancient language and how we can use it to our advantage.

In 1960, Richard Nixon and John F Kennedy were competing in the USA's first televised presidential debate. The more-experienced Nixon seemed to have the upper hand with his words, with listeners on the radio believing he had dominated the debate. But for the people who watched on TV, Nixon came across as less trustworthy and less confident. He looked tired, had stubble, grimaced and wiped sweat from his brow, whereas Kennedy smiled broadly and appeared calm and controlled. And with 70 million people watching, the difference in body language literally made all the difference. The result was that Kennedy came from behind to win the election, and for the following three campaigns, no sitting president would agree to debate a challenger on TV.

But you don't have to shy away from being seen. We have learnt a lot about how body language helped Kennedy win and, over the years since, countless studies have uncovered a few basic truths that you can apply easily. This is important, as before you've even spoken, your body position and movements may have already helped people to decide if you're to be trusted, liked and respected – it's said these decisions are made within just seven seconds.

Take a look at the illustration of various sitting and standing stances on the next page. OK, so these are pretty extreme examples, but even when dialled down to levels you're more likely to see day-to-day, it's easy to spot two distinct power types. Higher power (on the left side) tends to be expressed by expanding; more open, upright and forward-leaning poses. One of the classic high-power poses is the 'Wonder Woman' pose – hands on hips, chin and chest up, shoulders back. It signals confidence and leadership. Lower power is reflected by making ourselves smaller – shrinking – with closed, defensive gestures, a hand to the neck, slumped shoulders or looking at the floor. These signal ineptitude and insecurity. Which pose do you think will tell people that you and your ideas deserve to be taken seriously? Because even if you don't *feel* like a leader sometimes, you should at least appear to be one.

Power pose your way to power

Effective leaders can be calmer and more confident in stressful situations because they tend to have higher levels of a 'dominance' hormone (testosterone) and lower levels of a 'stress' hormone (cortisol) in their brains than other people. The confident poses they adopt (that we've just seen) are a result of these levels. But what if you could reverse engineer that power, what if you could *feel* like a leader simply by *posing* like one? That was the subject of a study by Harvard Professor Amy Cuddy whose resulting outstanding TED talk showed that your body language doesn't just *show* who you are – it also *shapes* who you are.

Cuddy found that adopting a power pose, like the Wonder Woman pose, for two minutes boosts testosterone by up to 20 per cent and reduces cortisol by up to 25 per cent. That's quite a shift in a short time! As a result, her test subjects became much more tolerant of risk and when they were put into job interviews, they were deemed much more employable than people who had done low power poses

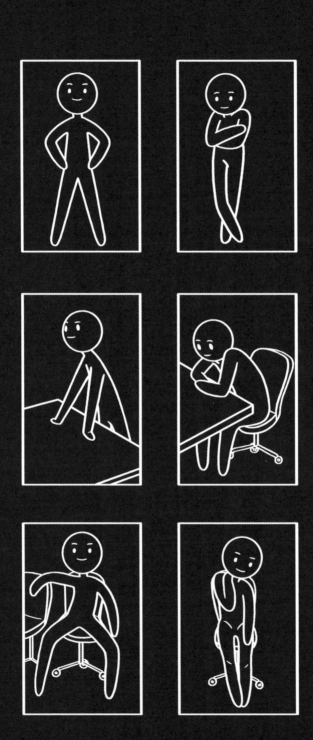

for two minutes. This wasn't because of any difference in what they said, but because of their presence; being seen as more passionate, authentic and confident.

When we're presenting or speaking in person, we naturally want to show we have the authority to be there. But what if we don't feel that ourselves? Well, firstly, 'imposter syndrome' is much more common than you might think. You are certainly not alone. You can be sure many of the people you see on stage that appear to ooze confidence will have been puffing their cheeks before they walked on. And secondly, you can try posing your way to power: Cuddy advises that before any important situation, find a private space, take two minutes to get into a power pose and you'll reconfigure your brain.

'DON'T FAKE IT 'TIL YOU MAKE IT. FAKE IT 'TIL YOU BECOME IT.' – AMY CUDDY

Adopting the body language of the person you wish to be will help you to become that person. And the implications go way beyond the stage – keep behaving like a confident communicator in every aspect of your communications and you will become a true leader, moving plans and people forward. As Cuddy says, **our bodies change our minds, our minds change our behaviour and our behaviour changes our outcomes**. Tiny tweaks can lead to big changes in the way your life unfolds.

The essential rules

Body language is essential for three main outcomes: **showing confidence, expressing meaning and building engagement**. As a leader you need to consciously take control of your body just as you command the words that are coming from your mouth. And you need to be able to read the meaning in other people's body language if you want to be in the best position to influence the way they think. Here are some rules to follow:

Posture

Our posture advertises our character. Power poses can help boost your mood but standing like a superhero for your whole talk or conversation might make you look more like Twatman than Batman; potentially appearing arrogant or even intimidating. As a general rule, when standing, adopt an open posture, upright, with your shoulders back. Then relax your shoulders to relax yourself. If seated, sit upright but not too stiffly, and lean slightly forward in your chair. Sitting upright indicates confidence and ease. Leaning forward indicates interest and involvement. Be open and take up space.

Face

People will spend a lot of time looking at your face so be mindful of what it says. This is especially important in this era of Zoom and online conferencing, when three quarters of our bodies are cut off by our screens. Most important: keep your hands away. Touching your face indicates dishonesty, covering your mouth suggests disagreement – which can cause the other person to become defensive before they've even finished their idea – and touching your neck or the back of your head indicates uncertainty. And when listening, tilting your head very slightly to one side indicates openness, whereas keeping it straight can indicate defensiveness or arrogance.

With 43 different muscles, our faces are capable of instantly contorting into countless expressions that reflect the emotions we feel inside. Anyone looking at you will quickly know if you're angry, sad, joyful or anything else and they will attach these emotions to the meaning of what you are saying, or – if you are listening – to how you are reacting. Reflect how you wish to be understood; look hopeful when you sell your idea and if you anticipate a negative reaction then mitigate it by signalling something more positive. So, if you think someone will be sceptical, express certainty and excitement, rather than mirror their unease. And keep reading their reactions – if someone looks uneasy, use your face to offer reassurance and comfort.

Eyes

Looking down at notes or a laptop makes you appear disengaged and looking down at your hands indicates a lack of confidence. Looking down when making important points can also suggest you are lying or that you fear your audience's reaction. If you want to forge a firm connection and signal trust, you have to maintain a good level of eye contact. But don't overdo it, staring non-stop signals serial killer! When presenting, eye contact doesn't lose any of its importance – you want every individual to think you are speaking to them. In a big room, it can help to divide the audience into six sections and move your eyes between them to ensure everyone feels they're getting your attention. If you're co-presenting, try and focus your eyes mostly on your partner as this will subconsciously direct the audience's attention to them also.

Smile

Leonardo da Vinci created arguably the world's most famous smile, so he knows a thing or two about them. He said, 'I love those that can smile in trouble.' And it's true – if we look downhearted then others will feel it too. A smile offers hope. And on a daily basis, in conversations, it shows engagement and empathy to others. It also fundamentally makes you feel more happy, energised and confident. All this makes you more likeable and people listen to and act on the words of people they like. You can channel your inner Mona Lisa by thinking of a happy memory and instantly the corners of your mouth will turn up. That's all you need.

Hands and arms

Never cross your arms, unless of course you want people to think you're aloof and hostile. And avoid fidgeting – this looks like a cry for help. If sitting, don't hide your hands under a table – it looks like you are hiding something.

Free your hands but use them purposefully – don't wave them about madly. Keep your gestures from your navel to your eye level and use them to emphasise key parts of your speech. You can indicate importance by gesturing to one side with an open hand, palm facing the audience. Or you can indicate meaning – show a number you are saying is small by pinching your finger and thumb and show it's big or significant by opening your arms and hands widely. You can also use your hands to express synergy or contrast: bringing your hands together indicates two ideas forming into one, and contrasting ideas can be shown by gesturing first to one side, then the other, literally placing the idea 'on one hand' and 'on the other hand' in the audience's mind. These might sound like blunt, obvious gestures but they work. Your body gives more meaning to your words, so use it.

Mirroring

Our ancient lizard brains feel happy when we see other people mirroring our body language. It helps establish rapport and capture our attention, which in turn leads the way for deeper conversations and connections. When your body fails to react, it can make the other party wonder, 'Are they even listening to me?' So adapt your body language (as well as your tone, of course) to the situation and who you are speaking to.

/BODY LANGUAGE SUMMARY

POSTURE: Be open and take up space, don't shrink. Adopt a power pose before speaking or a meeting then calm it a little when it's show time.

HEAD: Keep your chin up and hands well away to avoid looking dishonest or defensive.

FACE: *Show* the meaning and emotion of your words and display your reactions to their words to build engagement.

EYES: Keep good eye contact (but not stalkery levels) and in large rooms cast your eyes around so you connect with everyone.

SMILE: It goes a long way. It makes both you and them more positive about your ideas.

ARMS: No crossed arms, no fidgeting. Use gestures calmly and in a controlled way to emphasise points and give meaning to concepts.

MIRROR: Don't intimidate with a powerful pose if they're backing away into the bin. Show you get them by reflecting them.

/PERSUASIVE CONVERSATIONS

As The School of Life puts it in its book *The Emotionally Intelligent Office*, 'Ironically, the trickiest obstacles to communication continue to occur in what seem like the most favourable circumstances: when we're standing in a room close to another person who speaks, ostensibly, exactly our language.'

We long to be understood in conversations and yet we often don't invest the time it takes to help people understand. We mourn, 'Ugh. Why don't people just get what I am *thinking*?' This is despite the significance of effective conversations in *every* aspect of our lives; in relationships, with colleagues, in interviews, when buying or selling, and when trying to bring people around to our ideas. Poor conversations can lead to inaction, a lowering of respect and even conflict. Get them right, though, and, well, you know the score.

So what does it take to be dynamic and persuasive? Earlier, we ran through the 10 rules of behaviour change communications, which you will use to steer how you frame your ideas. These were *Clear, Easy, Positive, Beneficial, Relevant, New, Normal, Rewarded, Emotional and Visible.* And these, of course, need to be understood and applied when having conversations, as every conversation is trying to move people along the scale to advocacy. But here we will zoom in a bit on how to make a success of those 'favourable circumstances' of sitting in front of your subject of change.

Oh, and if you've been worrying that I may have run out of alliterative lessons, fear not and embrace **the 4 Cs of conquering conversations**.

Confidence → Connection → Clarity → Conversion

1. Confidence

Confidence is essential to being a convincing leader. And confidence comes from two main areas: first, from *believing* in what you are saying (having it rooted in your purpose) and secondly, from *knowing* what you are saying (by being prepared in advance). You then display your confidence by speaking slowly and clearly, with an assured tone and open posture.

Be prepared: You should never just jump into an important dialogue with a 'Hey, let's check in on this massively important thing and see what happens.' Your communication will be more persuasive when you prepare your intent and approach ahead of time. You might ask yourself questions like these:

What is your objective? Try writing this in a sentence.

What can you use to support that? Identify three key points (whether that's evidence or anecdotes) that will help to underline it or bring it to life.

What outcomes do you not want? Know what you won't settle for, a result that must be avoided, and think of ways you might avoid that.

Who are you speaking to? What are their values and desires, and the challenges they experience? Knowing this will enable you to be genuine, empathetic and relevant in how your idea is presented, as well as in your tone and language.

What are their beliefs? In what ways do you connect and differ?

How might you be challenged? First practice devil's advocate on your ideas then consider ways your ideas could be challenged by others. How will you counter that?

Such an approach will allow you to navigate even the most stressful encounters. Many of us find conflict so uncomfortable that we often avoid challenging conversations, or we sidestep challenging issues when they arise within otherwise ordinary conversations. By doing this, though, we are missing an opportunity to create real change, both in the world and in ourselves. Because the situations that are hardest to handle can create the greatest shifts. The result of avoidance can be misunderstanding, maintaining a dangerous status quo or resentment. None of these are desirable outcomes.

Be purposeful: No one buys into an idea unless they know why it exists. Just like no one takes instructions unless they know why they are being given. Persuasive communication puts the why at the centre. If the people you're speaking with align with this, they're much more likely to follow the idea through.

So when you outline your objective, make sure it is working towards your purpose. And make this purpose both understandable and relatable. Understandable means being tangible and real, an image they can recreate in their own mind. Relatable means it is something their own values can easily accept and connect with, so find the *part* of your purpose that speaks to their shared beliefs. When you can show your objective is supporting a bigger goal they also want – and not just your personal agenda – they're more likely to get on board.

2. Connection

Whether speaking to one person or a thousand, powerful communicators **establish a personal connection from the start**, before any messages are expressed, requests made or ideas suggested. We are focusing in this section on individual or small group conversations, but when you are speaking to a packed house, you should be just as emotionally genuine and give off the same feelings, energy, and attention you would one-on-one. If you ever turned to online yoga during lockdown and came across Adriene Mishler, you'll know what I mean. A smile, a friendly greeting, a joke and some words of encouragement and – despite many millions of others also tuning in – within a few seconds it's like an old friend is in your living room. The rest flows from here.

Rapport: Build that connection by being open, discussing shared connections and values, asking them about themselves and tuning into their conversation style, tone and body language – and then bring yours closer to this. This all helps to build trust.

Make it a safe space: If you want them to open up to you, they have to feel it is safe to do so. Convey respect, show their opinions are valued and express a genuine interest in who they are as a person.

Be human: To connect, you have to be human yourself. You have to show what drives you, what you care about. In this way, you create more opportunities for points of connection to form. And you have to show your vulnerabilities. When leaders are the first to admit vulnerabilities, it not only makes them trustworthy, it also opens the doors for others to admit their weaknesses and mistakes and thereby be accepting of ideas that could change their behaviour.

Empathy: Always consider the other's situation and how your words will be received. After BP's Deepwater Horizon well exploded in the Gulf of Mexico, 11 workers were killed and the resulting spill became the worst in US history: an ecological, environmental and economic disaster. BP CEO Tony Hayward had been rightly fielding questions for some time about the disaster and the clean-up, until one day he just broke and exposed the deeply insensitive nature of his personal thoughts: 'There's no one who wants this over more than I do. I'd like my life back.' The resulting furore over this callous remark led to his resignation. F*ck-up score: 10/10.

Emotional Intelligence (EQ): This is a hallmark of anyone who achieves influence. It refers to the ability to identify and manage your own emotions, as well as the emotions of others. It therefore goes beyond empathy. And the effects are far-reaching – emotionally intelligent leaders enjoy working with people who are far more engaged, productive and happy.

Professor Mark Brackett of the Yale Center for Emotional Intelligence offers a number of ways to develop your EQ, which I've distilled to the following points. Firstly, **Recognise and Understand:** Develop your awareness, to more actively identify your emotions and those of others, along with their causes and consequences (how they affect thinking and behaviour). 'You have to name it to tame it,' Brackett says. Then **Express and Regulate:** As a result, you can make more conscious decisions, matching your emotional expression to each situation to reduce, maintain or enhance the right emotions in yourself and others.

To pass an idea from our brain to someone else's requires that person to be receptive and that is not possible when they are scared, uncomfortable or angry. Often a discussion can end with each side more convinced of their point of view – not because of facts alone, but because of a feeling of having to defend themselves. Shouting may get people's attention but speaking with emotional intelligence gets support. In many conversations, we leave so much unsaid as we worry how we will tackle it sensitively. If you develop your EQ, you can discuss any topic in a fair and open way.

Engagement: Ensure the dialogue is two way, where both parties are fully involved. You shouldn't see this as your debate to win, but a chance to collaborate. If you go into a conversation thinking, 'They are wrong and I am right' you will never understand their position and how to shift that. We are more likely to commit to ideas that we don't agree with if we can participate in the discussion. So, be genuinely interested in the other person. Let them know you understand their motivations. Then show how you can help them.

Ask questions: The longer you talk in each exchange, the more your message gets lost in your own noise. You have one mouth but two

think
feel
DON'T

think
feel
DO

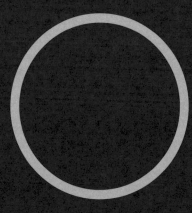

ears – make full use of them. Ask for more information or clarification as they talk to show you are paying attention and want to hear more.

Involve them: People want to be recognised so seek their thoughts and advice and thank them for their great ideas. And **send verbal and visual clues**: every 'right', 'uh huh' and head nod signals you are interested and encourages them to share more. Carol Kinsey Goman explains the power of inclusion in her book *The Silent Language of Leaders* like this: 'When others show us respect and appreciation, it triggers the same centers in the brain that are activated when we eat chocolate or have sex.'

Active Listening: Make a conscious effort to hear not only the words being spoken but also the complete message being communicated. Give them your full attention and note the tone, speed and volume. What is being said? And not said? Why is that? What hidden messages are in there? Don't start forming your response while they're still talking and jump in as soon as they pause for breath. **Listen. Then think. Then talk.** Please: never finish their sentences. You might think it signals you understand but it actually gives the impression you don't care to listen.

Back it all up with the body: So much meaning is conveyed with our hands, head and eyes. It's important that this meaning is backing up your objective. Your body language should underline the message of your words, as well as show engagement and signal your feelings when you are the listener. But if there is a disconnect between words and body, it can destroy trust. (See the Body Language section.)

3. Clarity

We often overestimate how good we are at communicating. We think that just because we've said something, we've been understood. Whereas, in reality, we are often too complex, assume too much or speak in an entirely different language. And when we do these things, we are not fully in control of the message. So...

Don't leave room for interpretation: We should assume as little as possible about the person in front of us. We often miss bits out of our speech as we think the other person can fill in the gaps, crediting them with knowing what's in our heads. When we do this in a one-to-one we may lose our connection. Now imagine the consequence of doing this to an entire auditorium, where hundreds of people each have a unique experience with your words... Don't imply a message, be direct.

'THE SINGLE BIGGEST PROBLEM IN COMMUNICATION IS THE ILLUSION THAT IT HAS TAKEN PLACE.'
– GEORGE BERNARD SHAW

Focus: When you're speaking to someone who jumps between topics like a fly evading a swotter, making random and rapid turns, it's hard to hook into their ideas or feel any motivation to act on them. You may even lose trust in their abilities.

Know the person: People draw on their backgrounds and past experiences to filter what you are saying into something that makes sense to them. Ensure your meaning survives these filters, by tailoring your language to the person in front of you. Use words to which they associate the same meaning and that are free from jargon.

Simplify: To make it easy to understand, you might break up more complex ideas into more digestible parts and build them up piece by piece. And you can use metaphors and analogies to connect your idea with things they already understand. Don't be lazy or clichéd when you do this though, like saying your idea is 'the Tinder of eco investing' – that example in itself is open to so much false interpretation.

Visualise: Create a visual image in their minds using rich language and stories, focusing on the positive effect the idea will have on them when it's put into action. They must be able to picture the change if they're to go after it.

Clarity is important as you have to get your message across first time. Questions are good but they should be the kind that show they are intrigued and desire a deeper understanding, not that they are confused and losing their confidence in you. And if they do want to go deeper, you have the answers to those questions already prepared, right?

4. Conversion

Get rid of the idea of a used car salesman with cheap tricks and mind games. Conversion – i.e. inspiring people to move from their way of thinking to yours – is about helping the person in front of you to reach their own conclusion that this is the right decision for them. To do that, the rules on behaviour change especially apply here. But let's keep zooming in...

'YOU CANNOT INSPIRE OTHERS UNLESS YOU ARE INSPIRED YOURSELF.'

– CARMINE GALLO, *TALK LIKE TED*

Frame it positively: People can get very defensive about the idea that they may need to change their ways. So make sure the conversation focuses on positive actions and positive outcomes. Inspire desire rather than guilt. Bring alive the passion you feel inside.

Lead with emotion: Information isn't what changes behaviour. You have to induce feelings to induce action, so access the emotional brain, then provide the reasoning.

Get them to say yes early on: In *Influence: The Psychology of Persuasion*, Robert Cialdini talks of 'Commitment', the idea that we humans have a deep need to be consistent. Once we've publicly committed to something, we're more likely to deliver on it. This principle works in broad ways – if you can get them to agree to something small, they're more likely to keep saying yes as the conversation goes on.

Then keep the yeses coming: People like saying yes more than no. It makes them feel positive and empowered. One way to apply this is to frame the conversation so that they make a series of 'micro compliances' – i.e. saying yes to ideas that are built incrementally to form one bigger action. The other is to steer a 'Socratic dialogue', one where the end decision is self-evident to them because they have agreed to all the reasoning steps before it, such as influencing your partner to want a pet: 'You like Lassie, right? So, you like dogs, right? So, we should get a dog ourselves, right?' OK, a few more steps than that may be needed.

Don't say no: Just as you don't want them to say no, you shouldn't say it yourself. It sounds defensive and disrupts the build-up of mutual positive intent. Instead, use phrases like 'I prefer to...' or 'In my experience, I find...'

Invite, don't tell: Ask questions that help them to reason out the answers for themselves. If you have provided enough context (emotional and factual) then a question like 'What do you think we should do with this project?' should lead to the same answer that you would give.

But now, they feel ownership and will activate it more meaningfully than if you just told them to do the task.

The audience is the hero, you are the guide: Remember, you are a small, green Jedi called Yoda. When you speak, make it less about you and more about what you can do for them.

Show the consensus: People want to know others are on board before they climb on, so show how the idea is supported. In a small group setting, identify the people who are most likely to adopt your ideas or who are already signed up and use them to lever the interest of others.

Create tension: When Seth Godin talks about getting someone to buy into an idea, he talks about creating *tension*. This doesn't mean making everything so stressful they just give in. It means engineering a desire to know more, like at the end of an episode in a drama series. Godin gives the example that if you say, 'Knock knock' to someone, they will reply 'Who's there?' They automatically want to know what comes next and consciously make that happen. When we create tension in how we express our ideas, by leaving gaps they can instinctively occupy, the receiver opens the door willingly rather than us having to bust our way in. So slow down your stories, allude to an emotion you are about to share, or create an engaging build up. Then pause. And wait for the 'Who's there?'

Offer a practical action: As with any communication there must be a call to action, so even if the dialogue is more conceptual, still have something they can do to show their commitment to the idea.

And be happy with progress: Don't get angry when people don't get it immediately or you'll make them defensive. It's unlikely you'll get a devout meat eater to become vegetarian after one conversation, but you can consider what could move them along the scale of action. Just try to ensure that in every conversation, something smart, positive or hopeful is concluded.

Reframe: Often, people reject ideas because of their limiting beliefs: 'I can't', 'that won't work', 'it's not for me', 'it's too hard.' So don't just inspire people to want to do something but also to feel *able* to do it. If you know the person's beliefs, you can use this to help find new paradigms, potentially even using their limiting beliefs to help them see something as new and attractive. For example, an adult tells you it is too hard to learn how to ride a bike. You might reframe it using:

> **Values:** *Imagine the life-long freedom you will feel once you've learnt to ride.*
> **Intention:** *The trickiness may indicate this is an important skill for you to have.*
> **Consequences:** *It will be much harder to get out of the city and enjoy the countryside if you don't.*
> **Underlying assumptions:** *You may think this as you are afraid of an accident, but research suggests it is safer than driving.*
> **Counter:** *I know someone who successfully teaches adults to ride in just a weekend.*
> **Analogy:** *Is there something else you learnt recently that you can share your experience of with me?*
> **Expansion:** *What do you mean by 'hard' exactly?*
> **Connection:** *Once you have learnt this, you will be a better learner at other skills.*
> **Bigger picture:** *If learning was too hard there wouldn't be millions of people riding bikes right now.*

(Hat tip to Ian Tuhovsky for introducing me to some similar ideas in *Communications Skills Training*.)

With any conversation, allow yourself to learn along the way. Why is this message not sticking? Why do people push back here? If you want a better outcome next time, you must try and understand how people react. Then you can influence many more people like them in future.

SKILL BUILDER: Understanding someone's personality type – how they respond to information and people – can provide a shortcut to knowing how to get the best outcomes from a conversation. Check out the short guide on my website.

A quick note on leading teams

A five-year study at Google found there are a number of characteristics shared by all effective teams, all of which rely on the leader being able to hold effective conversations (including embracing all the challenging ones). It's not just about who you work with but how you work with them that counts. Distilling the lessons to three points, they are:

Psychological safety: People feel free to share ideas, contribute and speak out, judgment-free, and they feel confident to express their vulnerabilities.

Clarity: Everyone has clear roles (and understands each other's) and they understand what is needed to reach their objectives.

Purpose: They understand how their work is having an impact and how it contributes to the wider company goals.

/PERSUASIVE CONVERSATIONS SUMMARY

CONFIDENCE: Build your confidence before you even enter the room by knowing *why* you are there (what you want to achieve through this dialogue – i.e. the objective) and *what* you are going to say (how you will frame your ideas based on what you know of the other person). Your objective must be working towards your purpose. And this objective must be understandable and relatable, with aspects they can connect to. Then display your confidence by speaking slowly and clearly, with an open posture.

CLARITY: Don't imply or leave room for interpretation. Misunderstandings lead to failure and even conflict. Make sure the idea is clearly expressed, built up with simple parts, visualised if possible and that you signpost where the conversation is going.

CONNECTION: Establish a connection from the start by using personality to build rapport. Ensure it's a safe space to share and test ideas and always show your own vulnerability as this will allow them to admit their weaknesses and be open to new ideas. Use your emotional intelligence to not only understand their emotions but to also affect them, and therefore make ideas easier to land. Ensure the conversation is two-way and interactive – actively listening and responding – as participation leads to buy-in.

CONVERSION: Having done all that, bring them over to your way of thinking. Don't tell them what to do, make them desire it by reframing negative beliefs positively, using the power of social proof, securing micro compliances (getting them to say bigger yeses) and creating a tension they feel compelled to open the door to.

/KILLER CONTENT

We are bombarded with messages all day from both people and organisations trying to 'sell' us an idea. The ones that stick are the ones that have been laboured over, rewritten, retested, refined and sent to us at a time of day we will be receptive, via a channel we are happy to consume information from – the ones that have been constructed consciously... for... us. But, crucially, the ones that really work are the ones that lead to us doing something.

We call the discipline of getting our content out into the world 'content marketing' or 'inbound marketing' because it's all *marketing* the promise of our brand and then driving *inbound* attention to us. Whereas we might put a press release out to the media and see what happens (as we'll see later), we use our owned content in a very tactical way to target our audience where they are, with what they care about, and make them want to come *in* to our world.

Content is such a cold, ugly word for what can be a magical and powerful expression of your ideas. The right content informs and inspires, it gets attention, and it gets shared. And whether it's an article, a video, a podcast or a speech there are five steps you can follow to make sure any content you produce is killer content.

Create → Design → Draft → Edit → Repurpose

1. Create – refine the idea

Before you start writing, scripting, filming, recording or doing *anything* to produce your content, you have to really drill down into what your idea is and what you will do with it.

For this step, we have to ensure six fundamental questions have been answered. These questions are **Why, Who, How, What, Where, When**. A lot of Ws and one H, so let's refer to them simply as the HWs from on. Let's work through each in turn...

WHY do you want to produce this content?
Yes, the why again. Before you decide what you're going to produce, you must be really clear on why you're going to do it at all. There must be a reason, something you want to achieve with it. It's not good enough to say, 'Because I haven't posted a blog for a while.'

Maybe it's to raise awareness, grow sales, recruit volunteers – you name it, there will be a bunch of things you need to do to further your objectives, to work towards your plan. If you're looking for funders, you might require content that showcases your deep knowledge of trends within a sector, to show you are a sound investment. But if you are a freelancer looking for clients, you might need to showcase technical understanding, to highlight the expertise you bring to your work.

The why should be the starting point of any communication – content writing, interviews, speaking, marketing, advertising or media relations.

WHO will you target with this content?
All your content must answer a core need in the audience; it must solve problems or speak to their desires, even answering their questions

before they are fully formed in their minds. So, what are they looking for, what will they respond to? Well, you have their profiles (page 36) to help here. Your knowledge of the audience will inform everything from the action your content pushes for and where you will place it to how you frame the idea and then how you craft the detail of the content.

HOW do you want them to act?
As you know by now, every single powerful communication you make will lead to a reaction (and hopefully an action) from your audience. So, be in control of what that is by working a clear ambition for action into your planning. Depending on the why, you might want people to sign up, show up or perhaps shape up. Identify what you want, as well as what's in it for them. Remember, any action must feel like something that is for them, not for you.

Important to note: Before we've even considered what we are going to focus on, we have started with *why* we will produce content, *who* we are targeting and *how* we want them to act. It is with this information that we can make a meaningful decision over *what* we will produce. Far too often, people start with a topic and try to retrofit why this is important to their objectives. The result? Crappy content.

WHAT will the content focus on?
Your thought leadership pillars (already in your canvas) should be the well from which all your ideas for content are drawn from. And you can use a number of ways to dive deeper into that well.

Your audience: You could focus on things they're concerned about and provide solutions for this or use their values as a starting point. But you can also put yourself in their shoes – hang out where they hang out – and see what sort of content they're consuming. Where is the clear space?

Your work: You will be sitting on a gold mine of ideas from the insights you have gathered, data you've collated and the success stories of your work. It's easy to think everyone knows this stuff. They don't. If a journalist was rummaging through your activities, what (positive) stories might they come up with?

Experience: You might also guide people with new things you learn – whether that's insights from a conference or takeaways from a course. Once you have finished this book, you may even want to package up your learnings and show how others in your network could apply them.

The future: You are guided by a vision of a better future, so reach into that future and pull in its stories. And show your understanding of the near future with forecasts and trend pieces – these can be popular, particularly at the start of the year or during a period of change.

The calendar: There are many established diary dates through the year that lend themselves to professional content. Think COP, Davos, Earth Day or even – my favourite – National Pizza Day. And then there are religious or cultural festivals and celebrations, such as Christmas, Chinese New Year or Thanksgiving, to name a few. By crafting useful content related to the themes of these dates, we can hack our way into the focused attention the subject is receiving and bond with our audience over shared interests.

The news: As well as making news (which we'll come on to), you can also tap into the news around you for content ideas. What's happening in the world that you can analyse or reflect on in a meaningful and helpful way?

As your focus starts to form, push yourself to be creative. Don't be satisfied with the obvious that anyone could come up with. Here are some ways you might **find a unique angle** on the topic:

- What has already been covered on this?
- What new aspects or unique insights can I bring to it?
- What other topics of interest are related to this?

- Why will the audience want this, how does it benefit them?
- What surprising, challenging or counter viewpoints can I use?

WHERE will the content appear?

Knowing where your content will be seen – on which channels or in which geographies – will further influence how you go about creating it. One idea might be represented very differently as a blog on your site than it might be as a speech in another country.

When deciding where it will appear, always try to earn the biggest opportunity first. So, if hardly anyone visits your website, don't write a ground-breaking article with the intention of leaving it there – think of how you could target the media or an influential stakeholder before you share it on your owned channels.

And don't forget those stakeholders. You need to think of some of them as being like a media channel; known and trusted by your key audience. Earlier, you listed your key stakeholders – you need to put these to work. They may have widely read newsletters, a popular YouTube channel, a guest blog or events you could speak at.

WHEN is it appearing and referencing?

You should be aware of what else is happening around the time you plan to issue your content – do you need to reference, acknowledge or connect with that? Or perhaps you need to move your timeline, so those other events don't get all the attention. And are there specific dates that actions from the audience need to occur on or by? Ensure all relevant time references are captured in your planning.

Great, you now have your idea. Kaboom. Next step is to capture it succinctly.

Write the idea as a sentence

When I was starting as a reporter, I found myself describing to my news editor some of the stories I was working on, in long, rambling ways. She told me to try again, this time imagining I was telling it to a stranger next to me on the bus. It was a simple trick but suddenly all the confusion and jargon slipped away, and I was able to present the core of the idea neatly in simple language.

If your idea isn't already formed this way, write it down as a single sentence. You must be able to express your idea this way as that proves you have really understood what is at the heart of it and how you will tackle it.

And capture your 3 Key Messages
We give the idea some form by expressing it as three key messages. Not two or four but three. Three gives the idea the scope needed to allow your idea to fulfil its objective but any more and its power will be diluted and people won't remember them anyway. These messages capture all the important points of your idea – what the idea is, why it's valuable and what we want people to do with it. So make these messages meaningful and memorable. And capture them succinctly so they can be tailored for different audiences.

'I KEEP SIX HONEST SERVING MEN, THEY TAUGHT ME ALL I KNEW. THEIR NAMES ARE WHAT AND WHERE AND WHEN AND HOW AND WHY AND WHO.'

– RUDYARD KIPLING,
THE ELEPHANT'S CHILD

We use this format – one overriding focus, three key points within that and then supplementary information that supports those points – as the basis for all killer content.

If you follow the HWs, you can ensure your content fulfils three important criteria: *it has purpose, it doesn't focus on yourself and it adds value.*

Let's imagine you've just won an award. You naturally want to tell the world. But how can that fulfil the three criteria? Instead of writing about the win itself, you might construct a piece around insights learnt from the project that was awarded so that others could benefit from your work. You could even use the voices of the people who you worked with to tell that story. You can still mention the win, but as just one of the messages, not the focus. The value of the content has just gone up considerably, as has the likelihood people will actually read it.

2. Design – organise the outline and structure

Aida is an opera by Verdi, a timeless story of passion, conflict and action. So, in many ways, it is like AIDA, a jargony term for how to use wonder and emotion to *compose* your content so it really *sings* (sorry!).

AIDA stands for: Attention Interest Desire Action. Whether it's video, audio or written, you have to grab the audience's *Attention*, spark their *Interest*, awaken their *Desire* and then, when they are fully primed, call them to *Action*. So include these ingredients:

Attention **New** – something unexpected and surprising.
& Intriguing – sparks their curiosity.

Interest **Relatable** – feels relevant, targeted at the audience's profile, and timely.
& Engaging – connects emotionally, is enjoyable and per-haps challenges them.

| Desire | **Inspiring** – helps them picture a shared future. |
| | **& Informative** – motivates them to want to act. |

| Action | **Useful** – shows them what they can do and how to do it. |
| | **& Empowering** – makes them feel able to do it. |

You should think about how you can create this effect through the structure of your content. Just as you might make a sketch before completing a painting, you should sketch an outline for your content. Give it a basic shape, noting where the key points you just identified will go and how you will open and close it.

Then, look at your structure and consider what knowledge, data or stories you can use to bring it to life, as well as the additional information you need to find to fill the gaps. Note all the audience's questions and make sure you can answer them.

3. Draft – produce quickly, without judgement

Whether you're producing an article, report, speech or video, chances are you will be writing it out first (at least in part). And when you do, it's important to produce your content quickly without stopping to question it, using your structure and key messages to guide you. If you've done the planning well, the writing should just flow. And if it doesn't, just write XXX where you get stuck on the right word or phrasing and jump to the next bit, so you don't hold up your flow. The same goes when you find you are missing info, data or names – just note where you need to do some extra research, then move on. Go back and fill in the blanks later.

And keep these rules in mind when constructing your content:

Two-way street: Ensure your content does more than broadcast. Engage people – not just to act but also interact, building relationships. People like to feel they're adding value themselves – is there a way to ask your audience to share their views or contribute inputs?

grab
ATTENTION

spark
INTEREST

awaken
DESIRE

call to
ACTION

Be authentic and consistent: Make sure you deploy the tone of voice you developed from your archetype. But be mindful of nuance and adjusting for the audience – scientists reading an academic review will require different language and structure to teens watching your helpful how-to.

Be visual: Every piece of content you produce should have images associated with it that summarise the messages and emotions of the content. Images make your content much more engaging and fundamentally more attractive; more likely to be read and shared. On LinkedIn, posts with images get twice as many comments as text posts, and videos are five times more likely to get comments. Select an image at the start and make sure it complements. People will be put off by anything that looks like it was bolted on for the hell of it, is overly photoshopped, contains a confusing mash-up of styles or is obviously a cheap stock image a hundred people have used.

4. Edit – check, fill gaps, reorder, revise

Editing is the secret to great content. It is often in this stage where the piece really comes together. As Stephen King said, 'To write is human, to edit is divine.'

Firstly, check it over straight away once, to see if it ties together, to understand where it could be simplified or strengthened. Then leave it, overnight if possible, to let the ideas ferment and build in your creative subconscious. Then... edit. Do this in three rounds if you can.

First check: Sense and structure. Make sure it is clear, concise and impactful. Is anything missing? Is there a strong opening and close? Are the key messages clear? Is it confusing or convincing? What can you trim? Where do you need anecdotes or humour to bring out personality? Is it really produced *for* the audience?

Second check: Detail. Errors and inconsistencies create doubt and mistrust in readers so check your spelling and punctuation (if the content will be written in its final form) and even facts. You don't want people to think, 'This person was so unconvinced by what they were producing they didn't even check it.'

Third check: Out loud and by someone else. Reading out loud can help identify patterns or gaps in the logic and emotional connection you couldn't spot when reading it in your head. Then, if it's a written piece, ask someone else to read it before you publish. If it's a video or audio piece, get someone else to take a look or listen. Be open to criticism, it helps you improve. But ask for structured, specific feedback. And see if they can pull out the three main points. If they can't, you're not being clear enough.

Great. The content is fan-bloody-tastic and it's ready to go live. But, wait, that's not the end of its journey.

5. Repurpose – make your content go further

If the idea is good, then be confident in that goodness. Consider how your content can be **repurposed** across other content types and channels. An article might also make a great short video, or be expressed in a simple infographic, as well as a series of visually led social media graphics, with each focused on a key insight from the piece. Or a talk may become a series of blogs. This repurposing helps widen the reach of your original idea, for little effort. I call this giving your idea **breadth**.

But there's another important aspect, related to how stories evolve over time, their **length**. Think back to any major news story. There is the initial breaking news, then there are **updates** on how the story unfolds, along with **analysis** about what it all means, **campaigns** launched on the back of the news, **forecasts** for what will now happen in the future, then there are **related news** announcements as the original news leads to new policies or behaviours, **features** looking

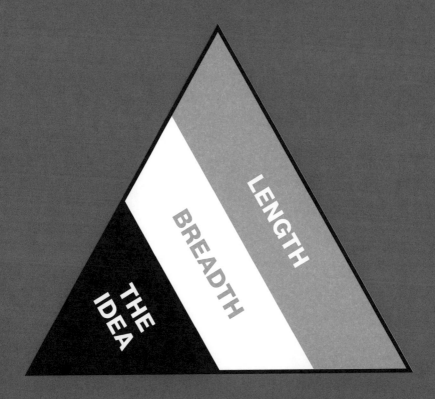

at the wider socio-economic impact of the news, human interest stories (**case studies**), **guides** on how to navigate the new reality... the list goes on and your idea can follow a similar evolution. By understanding this process, you can jump in with content at any stage. So always ask, 'How big can I make this idea?'

TO DO: **Follow these steps to produce a list of ready-to-go ideas (or half-formed thoughts you can return to). Keep these ideas in a 'content bank' folder and make a withdrawal when you need inspiration for content.**

SKILL BUILDER: **Find out how to build on this and ace your written content from page 168, and your talks from page 198.**

/KILLER CONTENT SUMMARY

CREATE: To find your idea, use the HWs: Why are you producing this? Who is it aimed at? How do you want them to act? What do you want to focus on? Where will it appear? When is it referring to? Draw inspiration for the focus of your idea from your work and the world around you, then find a unique angle on it. Ensure you can express the idea in a single sentence and as three key messages. The result should have purpose, be audience-focused and add value.

DESIGN: Organise the structure that will hold these messages. Create an outline that will perform AIDA – grab Attention, spark Interest, awaken Desire and then call the audience to Action. Note what further info or research is needed before you move on.

DRAFT: Produce quickly, without judgement, trusting in the structure and idea. And trust the process – the diamond will only shine in the next step. Use your tone of voice and audience profiles to steer your drafting decisions.

EDIT: Review, reorder, revise – editing is the secret to killer content. So check at least three times, including by someone else.

REPURPOSE: Make your idea go further by finding breadth (new content forms for the same idea) and length (new styles, approaches and angles based on how ideas evolve over time).

/STORYTELLING

Storytelling is the most important tradition we possess. For generations, we have been telling and passing down stories, each encoded with messages and moral guidance that help us to make sense of the world and find its shape. My two-year-old son's story books, for example, help him to understand why it's important to brush his teeth and care for animals, or just remind him that paper is not that tasty after all.

As Jonathan Gottschall, author of *The Storytelling Animal*, puts it, 'We are, as a species, addicted to story. Even when the body goes to sleep, the mind stays up all night, telling itself stories.' Our brains just can't get enough of a good story. And some of these stories have survived for millennia, such is their power to pass on information and create emotional connections.

In fact, those are two of the most powerful aspects of stories: they both protect the message and bring it to life. They take us to a new place, they influence our beliefs and help us to act on ideas we might otherwise have ignored for being irrelevant or confusing. They make ideas much more inspiring and easier to remember than facts and figures. They are our universal language as humans.

'THE UNIVERSE IS MADE OF STORIES, NOT OF ATOMS.' – MURIEL RUKEYSER,
THE SPEED OF DARKNESS

This is why so many great talks and speeches weave in, or even start with, stories. This is why we see them in pitches, in thought leadership articles, in adverts, blogs and reports. And this is why you must also now think of yourself as a storyteller.

So, what stories will you tell?

The stories that can bring our cause or ambitions to life are lying all around us. We have stories about our personal journeys, stories from the work we have done and stories that evidence, authenticate or explain how our ideas came to be and why they are so important.

The bike brand VanMoof uses stories to show off the distinct qualities of its products and services. For example, some of their bikes are equipped with smart technology and come with a 'we will recover your bike after theft or replace it' guarantee. But that sounds dry, so VanMoof tells stories. They created a video series called *Bike Hunters* where their team travels across the world tracking down stolen bikes using the GPS inside them. The stories – which consist of three parts: theft, chase and confrontation – reflect the disruptive energy of their brand personality and makes their promise totally clear.

Individual disruptors use the same techniques. Their stories are all creating new perceptions of the storyteller and vividly transferring their beliefs. And this can be an incredibly powerful force for change. Perhaps you know the old tale of the beggar who sat with a sign that read 'I am blind'. Few coins found their way into his hat until one day he changed the sign to read '*It's spring and* I am blind.' Now people passing were reminded of how much *they* enjoyed the cherry blossom around them and the birds returning. It told a story of sight. That small addition made a big difference to how people engaged emotionally with his struggle. His hat overflowed.

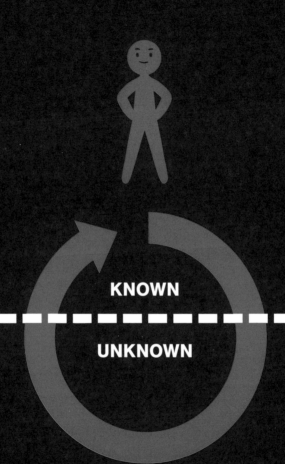

KNOWN

UNKNOWN

The shape of stories

Stories are always about transformation – an elemental moment of change – and this is exciting. When identifying your personal story earlier (in the Distinct chapter), we had a little help from the story form that's commonly known as the 'Hero's Journey'. We see it in everything from *Star Wars* to *The Lion King*. It helps us to describe a transformation that has either taken place (i.e. Simba journeys from cub to king, overcoming obstacles in his way) or can take place in the future, if the audience will allow themselves to accept our offer of change and *be the hero*. We guide them through the unknown.

There are other forms (or plots) to stories – such as 'Rags to Riches' (e.g. *Cinderella*), 'Slaying the Monster' (e.g. *King Kong*) or 'Rebirth' (e.g. *A Christmas Carol*) – but the Hero's Journey is the form you'll probably most commonly use, as a leader of change. Whichever plot you use, and just like the VanMoof example, your narrative of transformation is likely to consist of three acts:

1. **Challenge:** There is an obstacle that must be overcome or perhaps even a status quo that needs to be shifted.

2. **Solution:** The breakthrough, the alternative future or the answer to the problem is identified, as well as how to achieve it.

3. **Resolution:** We show what happens when this solution is applied, what our lives are like.

You can use a three act framework (which might also be expressed as *Situation, Action, Resolution*) for any story that you need to tell, whether that's to explain the value of your offer or to craft an anecdote that shows the impact you are having.

And using three elemental parts in all your stories doesn't mean they must be limited in their creativity. Far from it. You can play around with the structure and delivery to change the way you emphasise emotion, ideation or learnings, depending on *why* you're telling the story. There are a number of ways to do this. Here are six techniques (which I originally discovered through brand storytelling experts Sparkol):

False start: Start to tell a story, only to reveal surprising new information, then start the story again from this perspective. **Use to** surprise, shift perspectives, or show how you overcame failure or setbacks.

In media res: Start in the middle of the action, then spool back to how it began and what led to this. Give away just enough at the start to make the listener want to hear how it is eventually resolved. **Use to** grab attention or draw attention to a key point.

Nested loops: A story in a story (that may also be in a story). The central story contains your core message, and the others support this. The first story started is the last one finished, like unstacking and then restacking a Russian doll. **Use to** show how something is learnt through a series of experiences.

Converging ideas: Where nested loops have one central story and others around it, here you also talk about two or more elements but sequentially, and each one contributes to one lesson. **Use to** show how collaborations or movements started.

Petal structure: Multiple stories that each relate to one central message. Each story is independent, introduces the next and adds more emotion or evidence to the main idea. **Use to** have multiple viewpoints or multiple speakers support one idea.

Sparklines: Used by Nancy Duarte in her book *Resonate* to graphically map famous speeches, this approach emphasises the difference between the current world and an ideal world, contrasting *what is* with *what if*. It's what's applied so powerfully in 'I have a dream'. **Use to** build emotional connection with an idea. (See more on this in the public speaking section.)

The approach you choose will depend on your ambition and the situation. If you have multiple speakers, for example, a petal structure

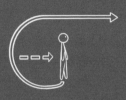

FALSE START

IN MEDIA RES

NESTED LOOPS

**CONVERGING
IDEAS**

**PETAL
STRUCTURE**

SPARKLINES

can help or if you want to recreate a moment of inception in your audience, you might first tell of how you came to make this discovery with a straight telling of a hero's journey.

As a supporter of Médecins Sans Frontières (MSF), I receive regular email updates on their work providing medical support to those most in need. Instead of dry reports and facts, they often share narrative updates. Here's one that instantly grabbed me:

'Operation Ebola: Dropped into the remote Congo with nothing but coffee, cookies and an experimental Ebola vaccine, nurse Trish Newport reveals how MSF's specialist emergency team took on the deadly disease.'

Immediately, there is jeopardy, personality, humanity, and something surprising. I click on the link and once I read this opening sentence, I am fully hooked.

'Just as we were opening the Ebola Isolation Unit, a pregnant woman arrived, transferred from another health centre. Within two minutes of being admitted, she went into labour.'

The writer makes full use of the *in media res* approach. I am pulled right into the action and by the end I am left wanting to get more involved with MSF's world. It does its job because it makes the important interesting. And it gives us a focus. There's a reason disaster movies follow one main character – we need human scale and human connection to access otherwise complex, enormous issues.

Ashoka, which came up earlier, also embraces the power of stories with its global community of societal changemakers. It understands how stories can help it to realise its vision of everyone becoming a changemaker. Martina Zelt told me, 'Rather than showcasing tales of distant heroes, we encourage our community to show the rocky and real path that led to them becoming changemakers. In this way, they can show others that they have the same changemaking power. Because they do. Everyone does.'

How to tell powerful stories

Pixar is renowned for its ability to produce memorable (and lucrative!) stories again and again. *Toy Story, Finding Nemo, Soul*... They do this because they have discovered the formula that works. And luckily for us, they've distilled this formula into 22 rules to follow (and if you want to check out the full list, Google is your friend). Some of the rules apply better to multi-character movies than they might to your needs, but many are immediately applicable. This is one of the most important:

Rule #14: Why must you tell THIS story? What's the belief burning within you that your story feeds off of? That's the heart of it.

So once again, we are reminded to start with the why. Your story must speak back to your purpose or there is no point in telling it. In the book *DO Story,* Bobette Buster captures this burning desire with the word **spark**. The thing you want to pass on can be thought of literally as a flaming torch. You hand the torch over to your audience and they use it to light their way in the otherwise dark uncertainty of the future. The first thing you need to do is find this spark as your story is the thing that is wrapped around it. The rest follows from here.

In crafting your story, you will of course apply the ideas we've been through on how to create Killer Content, but some points are worth reaffirming and there are a few new ones to add. So, to help you, I have created my own rules to rival Pixar's...

/10 RULES FOR STORYTELLING

#1: Find your spark: Your burning desire should be your starting point. This will help you find the story only you can tell. Stories from our own experiences are especially powerful.

#2: Determine the shift: What do you want people to do with this spark? Make this clear in the story. Remember AIDA: grab Attention, spark Interest, awaken Desire and call to Action.

#3: Capture your story in a sentence: Boil your story down to its essence. How would you describe it to someone on the bus, so they go 'no way!'? It must be clear, inclusive and worth repeating (so people will want to hear it again and tell others themselves).

#4: Know your audience: This story must be grounded in what you know of your audience if you are to pass on this burning belief with conviction, relevance and authenticity.

#5: Give it shape: Identify your three acts (e.g. *challenge, solution and resolution)* then play around with the structure and delivery to create something unique and powerful. Ensure you have your ending before you work out the middle, the detail that leads up to that resolution.

#6: Focus on people: Stories are about humans. Focus on an individual or small group, not a whole organisation. And make the audience care about these people if you want them to draw lessons from them.

#7: Show your personality: The story must reflect that you are also human and the way you tell it should reflect your personality. Think of how you want to be perceived.

#8: Bring out emotions: Express basic emotions such as frustration, happiness or hope and make the audience feel these too. Make them laugh and cry. Connecting ideas with emotions makes them more memorable. Remember Maya Angelou's words, 'People will never forget how you made them feel.'

#9: Zoom in on a detail: Change the pace and stir the senses by focusing on some small details, like the colour or shape of an object, a smell or sound, to make it real for the audience.

#10: Bring out the struggle: Every story must feature a series of challenges. The drama of victory over adversity makes it engaging. And because it requires the hero to change or learn something, it helps the audience to also believe in their own potential to change.

/WRITING

The right words can create magic. You land the contract, shift a policy, lead your tribe... That's because good, quality writing reflects the good, quality thinking that's going on inside your head and underlines why people need to pay you close attention. Get writing wrong, however, and it's worse than wasting your time – sloppy writing screams messy thinking and can discredit the very purpose you hold so passionately. So, you might say, it's pretty important.

You have probably written a bunch of things already today – emails, social media posts, reports, job ads, even birthday cards... As writing expert, Ann Handley says in her book of the same title, 'Everybody writes.' You are *already* a writer. And your skill in this area is only going to be more needed the more you grow your authority and influence.

Just don't expect your content writing to shine straight away. Writers through the centuries have painfully discovered that the first draft often stinks. Handley calls this **The Ugly First Draft** and I'm afraid you just have to accept this will happen to you. Embrace your ugly side and work through it – trust the inner beauty and personality will really come through later, and that this process will become easier the more you write.

There is nothing stopping you from becoming a writing superstar, in time. And, yes, thankfully there are some simple rules to follow. Just avoid the deadly sins...

Wait. Before you go on, make sure you have read the Killer Content section to understand the process of creation (from ideation to drafting and editing).

The Seven Deadly Sins of Writing

1. Defective

Your writing must hit its target. If it fails to get going, runs out of gas before the end, rambles all over the place on detours or fails to convince you what the whole point of the story is then it is defunct, doomed and a dud.

As readers, we make very fast judgements as to whether something is worth our time. So, when you plan the structure of the piece, organise it so all the essential stuff is up top. Open with the information the audience cares about most. Clearly demonstrate, 'Yep, this is for you!' And leave the least important bits for nearer the bottom (but not right at the bottom – that's the final call to action, of course). We sometimes refer to this structure as the inverted triangle, where the size of the section in the diagram represents the importance of the information it contains.

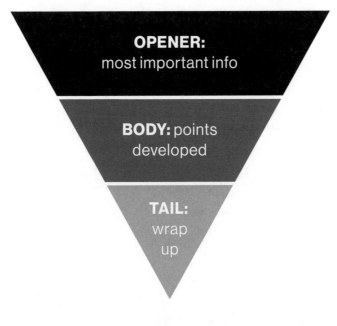

'THE FIRST DRAFT OF ANYTHING IS SH*T.'

– ERNEST HEMINGWAY

Another way of looking at this is: **Open with a punch, close with a kick.**

The opening punch: Grab them, explain your intention, set the tone. Once they're hooked, the rest is a lot easier. You might try and mix up your opening styles – a few to try include: enticingly summarise the story, ask a question, go big with mind-blowing data, jump into an anecdote, make a controversial statement or relay a familiar challenge the audience will relate to.

The closing kick: Never introduce a new idea at the end. Tie it all together to encapsulate your central objective. Make sure the questions, statements and intentions expressed at the start of the piece are neatly resolved at the end. Then kick it: you are writing for a reason, so end with something that moves the reader to perform your desired action (and make it very clear what that should be).

Remember AIDA. You have to grab their ATTENTION, spark their INTEREST, awaken their DESIRE, and call them to ACTION.

So what about those headlines?

Headlines are an essential part of ensuring your writing is not defective. Boring, long or confusing headlines will mean it's both the first and last thing people see. Make it count.

Sell the story: In just a few words, you need to convey your angle and express the tone. It must connect to and sell the rest of the story, indicating the newness, relevance and urgency. No easy task, especially when you need to...

Keep it short: There's a saying that 'six gets the clicks' meaning that shorter headlines are more likely to get an online reader's attention. Make it easy to skim.

Use striking word combinations: Use common, easier words to create the structure and less common words to add interest, ensuring these express emotion and power. Try some word play with alliteration, rhyme or repetition, or add odd numbers (odd numbers seem to grab the eye much better than even ones – a rule I have tried to consistently break through this book), which all engage the reader's brain. Create some Seth Godin-style tension.

Play with the format: Consider how you could improve engagement and shares by rephrasing your headline as a question ('How can we...'), list ('7 ways to...'), provocation ('Why you need to...') or guide ('How to...'). But avoid sensational clickbait that fails to live up to expectation – people won't be back to be fooled twice.

When you're reading other content, make a note of the headlines that grab you and understand why. You might even take one of these and just switch a couple of words as the basis for your own.

2. Difficult

Good copy should not be difficult. It should be *easy* to read, *easy* to understand and *easy* to act on. Most of us are not vying for Pulitzers but for persuasion. Words are there to transport your ideas and feelings so cut the excess and energise every word – think of your writing as being like a superhero's outfit – 'tight and bright'.

Get to the point: Readers (i.e. us humans) have small attention spans. Place the most important stuff at the start of each sentence. Cut the preambles, avoid over-intellectualising or philosophising. Just make your point and then move on. If you ever find yourself writing 'In other words...', ask yourself why you needed the first words. Think of your sentences as taking off vertically like a drone, not after a long runway with a groan.

Make it understandable: Use the words people really use, not medieval exhortations ;-) If you have to use an obscure word, explain it. Always err on the side of making it too simple rather than too complex.

Brevity is beautiful: Shorter words keep the reader engaged and show confidence. So... *remuneration = pay, utilisation = use, sesquipedalian = bad writing.* If you can use one word instead of three or four, do – it is more active. *Bring to a resolution = resolve. Give a response = respond.*

This applies to sentences and paragraphs: As a guide, sentences should be under 20 words and paragraphs just a few sentences. (But be sure to also mix it up a little – break up the rhythm to keep their eyeballs entertained and to sound more natural, like speech.) The job of every sentence is to get you to read the next sentence. And paragraphs are no different – they are bridges to what lies before and after, as well as self-contained islands of one thought. When considering the information each paragraph will contain, think of the reader – what do they need to know next?

Avoid padding: *It's often said that... It's important to bear in mind that... Interestingly... Surprisingly...* Just tell me already!

'SAY CLEARLY AND CONVINCINGLY WHAT THE ISSUE IS AND WHAT YOU WANT TO ACHIEVE. WITH EVERY SENTENCE ASK YOURSELF IF YOU'RE ADVANCING THE CAUSE.' – BRYAN GARNER, *BETTER BUSINESS WRITING*

Complex language confuses. Imagine if the news reported as follows about a man whose parachute didn't open: 'He experienced a sudden deceleration trauma as the consequence of a system failure in his personal aeronautical canopy.' No. So how should you do it? Writing expert Nick Parker – who is the founder of the aptly-titled That Explains Things – likes to give the example of a low hanging sign placed about 100 ft before a bridge in some small American town. It states, 'If you hit this sign then you will hit that bridge.' Simple and effective.

3. Dense

Density not only comes across in the words but also how they are visually presented. If your reader runs into a thick wall of text, they'll be knocked unconscious or at least zone out. You need to provide small clues and signs to guide them along, such as:

Use bold text to **highlight especially important words and phrases**. But use this sparingly; if you highlight too much text, **nothing will stand out**.

- Use bulleted and numbered lists: It can lift important information, simplify complex ideas and break up long chunks of text. But try to limit your list to five bullets.

Use subheads

Subheads allow you to cluster thoughts and break up text, making it easier for the reader to skim and digest. But keep them clear and informative.

Use Hyperlinks Wisely to connect to other related web pages. Hyperlinks – being coloured and underlined – can even act as a highlighter, so link the bit you want to stand out.

You can use rare single-sentence paragraphs to show off really important ideas, like this one.

Then... use subtle transitions to guide the reader – *then, although, still, therefore...* They help to keep the reader moving along.

Importantly – be consistent in how you present and break up your text. Don't make it look as confusing as the mad array of words above.

4. Dull

Surprise people, stand out, shake things up. Just, please, **don't be boring** – that just leads to snoring. **Tone** should reflect your unique brand personality, of course, but it should also always be human and popping with passion. Don't confuse formality with authority. Engage the audience and draw them in. When we speak, so much information is conveyed in our movements, gestures, pitch or pacing. With writing it's much harder to add character, which is why our tone of voice is so important.

Speak to the audience directly and inclusively, using *we* and *our* and *you* and *your.* And make it clear what's in it for them. **'Sell the prospect, not the product'**: if you're trying to flog drills, you're really selling the holes they make. It's the same with good copy – it should get across the opportunity for the reader; the problem you solve or the desire you fulfil.

'Quotes can also add colour to a piece,' someone probably once said. They break up the rhythm and add valuable third-party perspective on what's being said. So consider what other voices you can bring in, especially respected and influential people. Try and ensure your quotes are all one paragraph long (succinct, with every word working hard), that they serve a purpose (supporting the intended outcome of the piece) and that they add something new (complementing, not summarising).

5. Dead

Great writing is clear but stimulating, interesting but accessible, useful but enjoyable. It moves us, both emotionally and physically. It should be lively and a joy to read, so keep it active and convey a sense of momentum in your writing.

One obvious way to keep it alive is to avoid the 'passive zombies'. The passive voice is used on occasion for emphasis (like just then) but we need to cut back. The passive distances us from the words and their intentions, as well as from the person doing an action ('It is recommended...' is much less personal and powerful than 'We recommend...'). The way to spot the passive is to ask 'Can I add 'by zombies' after this?' If so, make it active.

> **The product was launched...**
> **The prize has been awarded...**
> **The writer will be eaten...**
> **– BY ZOMBIES!**

Dead writing also lacks conviction. People will only act on what you write if you inject some passion. Ann Handley, mentioned earlier, gives an example of when she was trying to get rid of her couches, which she admits were 'the exact colour of the poop emoji'. When she put up an ad offering 'Two free brown couches' she got no offers. So she tried again with this:

PUMPKIN SPICE COUCHES x2: Two upholstered gently used love-seats in a rich caramel hue. Deep, comfortable seating. Generous arm with sturdy back pillow supports. Perfect for binging Netflix or cozying up with your bestie on a chilly autumn night. From a smoke-free, pet-free seasonal cottage. Sad to see these go! $95 for the pair. These won't last!

It's a small but mighty example. She triggers your senses – making you imagine the sight, smell and feel of her crappy couches. She avoids clichés, evokes emotions, makes it personal and playful, transforms a negative association for brown into a positive one – the pumpkin spiced latte – and she uses storytelling (we can just imagine ourselves curled up on them watching TV). And she makes them desirable by establishing the value, not giving them away for free. The result? They sold quickly and for above the asking price. (By the way, that extract first appeared in Ann's brilliant newsletter *Total Annarchy* – and is used here with her kind permission. I encourage you to check out more of her work at annhandley.com.)

'THE TRUTH IS THIS: WRITING WELL IS PART HABIT, PART KNOWLEDGE OF SOME FUNDAMENTAL RULES AND PART GIVING A DAMN.'

– ANN HANDLEY, *EVERYBODY WRITES*

6. Djargon

Sadly, there's no equivalent for jargon that starts with a 'D' so I had to invent a new word with a silent first letter. It might catch on. It might get so well used it even *becomes* djargon. In fact, djargon represents jargon better than jargon represents jargon because you don't understand djargon. Confused? Exactly.

Use jargon and you might as well be speaking an alien language. Cut the twaddle, the claptrap and the gibberish. Write how people speak, or they will not hear you. Write like a human, not an institution, if you want to connect with your audience.

The two main types of jargon are *general bullshit* (widely used non-sense) and *specific bullshit* (used by your closer circle of friends and colleagues). For the first kind: you want to *socialise* that thought? Need to *circle back* on the proposal? That's fine if it's to a colleague who is programmed the same way as you, but not when speaking to earthlings. And for the second: all those weird and wonderful phrases that are unique to your world, like the 'D7 protocol'? Keep them there and translate everything into everyday language before it goes wider.

You should never use foreign phrases, scientific words or jargon when a simple word exists. And idioms – like 'piece of cake' or 'up in the air' in the English language – can also be confusing or alienating for readers for whom your language is their second language. Even some phrases that you feel are well established may benefit from some unravelling. For example, instead of 'systems change', you might say 'changing the structure of the things that make the most difference, such as the food or transport systems', at least in the first instance.

In 2019, The Guardian newspaper stopped using the term 'climate change' as it didn't capture the unnatural and urgent issues at hand. It instructed its writers to use 'climate chaos' or 'climate breakdown', which better convey the truth of what is being stated. The words we use are important. So check yours really convey the sense you are trying to express.

George Orwell wrote in 1946 that 'the present political chaos is connected with the decay of language'. He was reflecting on the effectiveness of Nazi propoganda in the Second World War, which had been using all means of communication to 'deprive its objects of the power of independent thought.' Three years later Orwell showed how far this idea could go with his novel 1984. Over 70 years after it was first published, that book could be speaking of the world we see around us today – with reality and fantasy being blurred, and suppression of our ability to do what is best for ourselves and the planet. As Orwell points out, we must continue to fight this by being mindful of the way we use language and – his key point – it must be simple. Orwell said: 'Deliberately misleading language is used to conceal disagreeable political facts.' We must hold others to account when they do this and communicate clearly ourselves.

7. Dumbass

Grammar is essentially the difference between knowing your shit and knowing you're shit. You don't have to be chief sub editor at The Times, you just need to understand the basics of how grammar works and how it helps us to communicate effectively. Mistakes happen, which is why we always check, check and check again. But sloppy or mixed-up grammar decisions can be wholly avoided by understanding the pitfalls. **Here are some common things to watch for:**

- US or British English: There are a few differences in words and spellings so pick your side and then stick with it. Don't mix them up in the same piece.
- Oxford commas? The stealthy comma before 'and' in a list. Pretty standard in the US, less so elsewhere – just be consistent.
- Avoid ALL CAPS: It's like shouting and it's what people do who can't express themselves with words.
- Cut down the exclamation marks!!! (for the same reason!!!)
- Watch for the apostrophes: It's, its; they're, their, there...
- And the homophones: Principal, principle; compliment, complement...
- Consistency: If you start using % don't introduce percent or per cent, if you write 'Book Titles' in inverted commas, don't then later refer to *Book Titles* in italics.

Sometimes, the dumbass mistake can lead to humorous effects. I spotted this genuine headline in a UK newspaper: 'Charity refused to help fox attack family.' Anyone missing a hyphen? But sometimes they can lead to serious offence, as well as reputation and financial loss. The publishers of *The Pasta Bible* cookbook had to destroy thousands of copies (and make some serious apologies) when they discovered that instead of 'freshly ground black pepper' in one recipe, it had stated 'freshly ground black people'.

Search Engine Optimisation (SEO)

What's the point in producing all this amazing writing if no one finds it? It's beyond the scope of this book to go into detail here but, top line, SEO is an attention to the language (**keywords**) people use when searching for answers. To be more visible to search engines you should use keywords throughout your writing and headlines.

A tool like **Answer the Public** (answerthepublic.com) can help you identify relevant keywords by showing what people are searching for around your specified topic. Or use **Google Trends (**trends.google. com), which analyses the popularity of search queries across regions.

When using keywords, **think in questions.** After all, we don't just search for single words, like 'clothes', but we might search for 'where can I buy upcycled fashion?' So use words from that phrase – or that entire phrase – in your content. And **use synonyms**: we use a variety of words for the same thing, so stick your keywords into thesaurus. com to find other options.

Google's algorithms (the codes that decide which pages come top of search results) prioritise content by the EAT acronym – content that shows **Expertise, Authority and Trustworthiness**. Apply these qualities when writing articles (or even website texts).

Style Guide

As the online bank Monzo says, 'Every word adds up to people's perception of who we are. And if the way we communicate confuses, frustrates or scares them, we can lose their hard-earned trust in seconds.' Monzo uses a style guide to ensure anyone communicating on its behalf can follow a consistent approach. You can do this too, for yourself or your organisation. Hopefully you already started your style guide earlier when noting your tone of voice and visual style. You can add to that now with rules to ensure grammatical consistency. Alternatively, you could just borrow someone else's style for these points. The Economist's Style Guide is great for this. Get a copy of the book and then pair it with your own needs: adding your list of keywords, the main concepts you use and how you explain them in everyday terms, as well your 'djargon list' – words you must avoid.

/WRITING SINS SUMMARY

DEFECTIVE: What is your idea and angle? Who is the audience? What do you want them to do? Answer the HWs before you type a word. Then start with the headline and ensure you have a structure that will open with a punch and close with a kick.

DIFFICULT: Good copy should be easy to read, easy to understand and easy to act on. Break down and explain your ideas. Words, sentences, paragraphs – all short and energised please. Keep it tight and bright.

DENSE: Don't knock the reader out with a thick wall of text – use formatting, headings and images to tell and sell the story more engagingly.

DULL: Sell the prospect not the product. Get across the opportunity for the reader. Apply your tone of voice and inject your personality.

DEAD: Persuasive writing is lively and popping with passion, so have conviction and keep it active to keep them interested. Kill the zombies!

DJARGON: (Yes, a silent D...) Write like a real human not an alien or institution, if you want to be heard, if you want to connect.

DUMBASS: Ensure a consistency of style and avoid sloppy and silly mistakes by knowing grammar pitfalls, having a style guide to refer to and triple checking what you write.

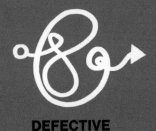

DEFECTIVE

DIFFICULT

DENSE

DULL

DEAD

DJARGON

DUMBASS

/PR & MEDIA

There's a huge difference between *you* saying your idea will help change the world and a source that people already trust saying it. This is especially true when that source is read, watched or listened to by thousands or millions of people. But what does it take to disrupt and dominate these sources of information? We need to get to grips with Public Relations.

To paraphrase the Chartered Institute of Public Relations, PR is about reputation; it is 'the *planned* and *sustained* effort to establish and maintain goodwill and understanding between you and your audiences.' As such, PR covers a broad scope of disciplines, all aiming to create the environment in which we can shape people's perception of us and, ultimately, their behaviour. But instead of examining all of these disciplines, here we are going to focus on the one that provides the biggest and most accessible opportunity, and is often synonymous with PR in its entirety, *media relations*.

Despite the ever-changing ways we source information, media relations can still be incredibly influential. One great piece of coverage could open doors to new audiences and give you something very impressive to share in your networks. And great coverage leads to more great coverage, as others see the signal that you have something worth paying attention to.

To get this coverage, there used to be just a handful of mainstream titles to target. But now the options are endless – from special interest websites and blogs to influential podcasts and YouTube channels. When you think of 'media relations', you should think of all these as comprising 'the media' and handle them the same way: you need to know who they are and how to get them to talk about you. That said, don't forget those old mainstream stalwarts because whilst fewer people are checking out newspapers (in print or online) directly, their stories still get massive traction when shared around on social media. Getting your story to the traditional media can therefore mean getting it to the source of the influence flow.

So how do you create a media story?

In *The Simpsons,* Homer's dad once appeared in a newspaper story with the headline 'Old Man Yells at Cloud'. The complete lack of significance of the story infers that dressing something up as news is easy. If only it were. You have to *craft* news stories – they should do all the things killer content does but with the emphasis on the *informing* part. And you only get to inform people if you really have something new to tell.

Stories that just aim to 'raise awareness' or are for the 'public good' alone are rarely, if ever, successful. You can't send out a press release on World Cancer Day that only reminds us of how many people are affected by cancer as – despite being tragic – it is not 'news'. That is a fact that you may use to underline your real news angle, which could be a new treatment, new data on shocking waiting times or new guidance on how to spot it early. Something... *new*.

You are probably sitting on top of a few great stories right now: stories of innovation, launches, overcoming challenges, successes, milestones or data. And there are probably a bunch of moments like these coming up in the next few months that you can start to already plan around.

But note that often the thing that the public – and therefore the media – will be interested in is not necessarily the same as the thing you're most interested in. This is especially true of reports. The media is bombarded with press releases every day with headlines like 'New report published by X' (as if the act of publishing is more important than what the report found) and journalists find themselves asking 'So what?' and not reading another word.

I've worked before with Circle Economy, a leading sustainability consulting and research organisation. When, in early 2021, the team published their annual stock take of how sustainable the world's economy was, they could have treated it like any other report. There was so much rich material they felt was valuable to share, but it needed simplifying into something the world could comprehend. Instead of dry and complex, they went with, 'Circular economy strategies can cut global emissions by 39%'. With the subheadline, 'Efficient resource consumption can save 22.8 billion tonnes of carbon and help avoid climate breakdown'. It's powerful and punchy, and taps into a narrative people already understand, the climate crisis.

That was the wow, the bridge into the rest of their three key messages, namely 1. This is what the data tells us (explaining what these big numbers mean to everyday folk), 2. This is what we need to do to improve (giving a sense of optimism and practical ownership to the reader), 3. This report is part of our wider work on this topic (oh, and by the way, we are available to work with you). The result was coverage in media outlets across the globe.

To create your story, use the guidance in the Killer Content section to find your idea and three key messages. These messages might simply focus on the *Announcement, Solution* and *Call to Action* of your news. The idea must be concrete and clear, not complex and confusing. Now tell that idea to someone else and see if they say, 'So what?' or 'What the hell?'

Jumping into the media cycle

Remember, you don't just have to wait for your own news to be part of the news. You can also thrust yourself into the cycle as a, yes, thought leader. When news stories are evolving, the media will always need expert voices to guide their audience. You might help to de-jargon something technical, or outline how things will play out next, offer advice on what people can do or share a story that brings the news to life in a novel way. You might find that your ideas are best suited for your owned channels – such as your website – or posted as a thought piece on LinkedIn, but always try and consider how the ideas you come up with could be used *first* by the media.

We did this effectively with one former client when a health crisis broke in the UK a few years ago. It happened between Christmas and New Year, meaning many other PR professionals were taking a break. Though the issue was not of our client's causing, we saw an opportunity to jump into the comment vacuum and establish their voice as the reassuring authority. Through statements and advice, we helped shape the narrative, educate the public on safe action and steer ideas for future policy. The media never forgot how helpful we'd been, and they never stopped coming back for more. That's because...

It's called 'relations' for a reason

The journalist receiving your idea for a story must know who you – or your organisation – is. And if not, you will have to work even harder and faster to sell the significance of why *you* are contacting them. So the first thing to do is to build relationships with the media so that when you need to get your story out, they will be receptive.

Step 1: Build your list

You need a working media list of titles and contacts to target. Start by asking which media / journalists your audience already goes to for their stories, and which have covered stories on similar themes. If you've completed your audience personas, you will already know the first answers. For the second, start monitoring: use google news searches and then set up news alerts (google.com/alerts) for your chosen topics, to keep a live track on what's happening in your field.

Create a spreadsheet. Capture the names of the titles and contacts, with all their contact details. Often you can find these contact details on the media's website or on the individual's social media bio. Do what you can to get a specific contact – if you pitch to general addresses (i.e. news@website.com), it will probably get lost or be seen as unimportant. And **don't overlook freelancers.** They have to pitch stories to the media to earn their crust so will not only be open to your pitch but will also be honest on whether your story is *actually* a story.

Within your titles, list the very specific opportunities they have, such as a weekly column, a monthly Q&A section, a profile page or anything else you could see yourself appearing in.

Now segment the list to make it more manageable. You might do this by scale / geography (such as international, national and local media) or by topic (such as into your three thought leadership pillars) or a combination. Within these, cluster the contacts by type – TV, radio, print and online etc. However you segment your list, make sure you **highlight your top tier targets**, the ones that have greatest relevance and opportunity.

Step 2: Build the relationships

To ensure you're on their radar, feel free to reach out and say hi to your top tier targets. Introduce yourself and show them how your work is relevant to their interests. Tell them you will be sharing some exciting news with them in the future, but for now you are available if they need help or commentary on your listed topics.

Continue to make them feel special by sharing helpful content when you spot it and by inviting them to events with no expectation on them. Engage with them on social media – it's there you will really see what they're passionate about and what they're working on. Sometimes they will use Twitter to make a request for help with a story. If so, jump in and advise, even if that means pointing them to someone else. Show how valuable you can be. And when they do cover you or meet with you or if they just write something relevant, keep a track of all this in your media list. That way, you can refer back to it when you next make contact.

Pitching your story

Effective media relations means being tactical and targeted, not shooting out a mass email and hoping for the best. You have to sell your story in your email pitch.

Journalists are looking for something...

Personalised: Make it clear why you are approaching them specifically. Show off your knowledge of their work with something like, 'I see you cover this topic in the Changemakers section of your weekly newsletter and have prepared all the information for you.'

Clear: Journalists have little time and are bombarded with hundreds of ideas a day, so show some understanding – be direct and concise. Make it very clear what the story is and why this is an opportunity for them. That means specifying its news value, timely relevance and significance for their audience.

Easy: If the journalist has to do lots of work to ask for missing information, to decode your technical language or anything else that requires precious brain space then you've lost them. Have everything they need, ready to go. Make sure images and other visual assets are ready and approved, spokespeople are named (and briefed) and case studies are written up.

In advance: Give them enough time before the story's go live date so they can plan how they will cover it, then follow up a couple of days before that date to give them a nudge.

How *not* to pitch

The BBC's technology writer Rory Cellan Jones is inundated with press releases every day. And lucky for us, he shares some of the worst pitches on Twitter. Here are two of the milder fails:

Following on from my email yesterday, our CEO will today be performing a Christmas charity 'stunt' whereby he will be livestreaming himself saying the word 'crypto' 100,000 times.

I wanted to get in touch with you to introduce my new client and to see if there's an opportunity to collaborate on editorial. We're seeking profiling Q&As, expert style commentary and product round-up opportunities with like-minded publications.

You might think these are innocent enough but approach like this and they will never open your emails again. Both offer no news, have no relevance, *ask* rather than *give*, and they assume the BBC will just 'do them a favour' and write about them. Er, no.

How to pitch

Dear [name],
I am contacting you from [give a top line on your organisation, if relevant].
Please find below a story that we are announcing on [add date, and relevance of date if needed].
[Summarise the story key points to show the wow].
I thought it would be of interest to you given [add in relevance related to their work and / or the current news agenda].
I can also offer you [add in details of assets, such as photos, graphics, a report, further interviews etc].

Please let me know how I can help further.

Paste the press release below the email. Play around with this pitch format to find what works for you and the opportunity. And make it clear if you are offering anything exclusive as this will make them more interested.

You should focus your time on your top tier targets, of course. The lower priorities can receive a more general email but even then, address each directly, never send out a mass email with your contacts in bcc. That is the way to the spam folder of doom.

How to write a press release

Fewer journalists now rely on press releases (hence why relationships are so important). But press releases can still be very helpful for announcements and coordinated activations. They also help you to ensure you have really got to the essence of your story, given how structured they are, and you can then use your releases as the basis for other activities – stakeholder briefings, thought leadership articles or videos.

Sometimes the media will take your press release and use much of it as it stands but more often, they – especially quality media – will rework this information, using it as the basis for an original take on the story. They might conduct additional interviews, source more data or feed your story into something bigger. So a good press release should present all the relevant information accessibly and simply so they can work with it how they need.

Headline: The obvious (but often overlooked) starting point... what is the headline? If people don't connect with this, they will probably not read anything else. It should summarise and spark curiosity (see page 171 for more on headlines). Consider a subheading if you need

I can
help you

↓ ↓ ↓

MARKETING

Trust me, she
can help you

↓ ↓ ↓ ↓

PUBLIC RELATIONS

to expand on the headline, or you might use three bullets under it to outline the three key summarising messages of the story.

Structure: Make sure the story is clear within the first sentence, and that the most important information is near the top.

Formatting: Format the text so it's easy to skim and digest. Break up blocks of text, use bulleted lists, quotes and bold headers.

Call to action: Always provide a next step for readers. It should be included early in the release, then repeated at the end, with a relevant web address.

Quotes: Include quotes to add credibility and to provide usable soundbites. Include one or two different quotes of one paragraph each. As press releases should be factual – and because they are written in the third person – you can use your quotes to express any opinions that do exist.

Word Count: Keep it brief and succinct; aim for around one side of A4 and never more than two.

Proofreading: Your press release is doomed if it contains spelling mistakes and grammatical errors. Always have a proofreader. Better still, two.

Additional info: At the end of the release, write 'Ends' to show where news stops and supplementary info starts. Below this, add in your contact details, website URL and what else you're offering (see next page). And include your boilerplate – this is a condensed description of you or your organisation; your *why how what* in one paragraph. You can use your value proposition here.

What else do you need for your media package?

Visuals: Given the fact the story will appear online and the media are also competing for eyeballs, you need to help them make it stand out. Having images ready makes the journalist's job a lot easier and therefore makes them much more likely to cover it. Good images strengthen the message, help to tell the story, visually summarise, captivate and engage, are immediately understandable and motivate action. Make sure your images are high res, in both portrait and landscape (so they have options), are captioned (with all people in the photo named), and that the appropriate credit is listed.

Assets: You may have other materials that the media will find useful, such as a report or an infographic. And you should always have case studies, complete with photos. The media will need real human stories that help explain or embody your news.

Stakeholders: How can you involve your priority contacts? Can they provide a supporting quote? Or can your contacts at least help get the story out? Share the story with them, along with the visuals and assets, and even suggested social media posts.

Q&As: Consider all the follow-up questions the media may ask after they read your story and have answers prepared for these.

Examples to check out

The company pr.co provides fantastic online newsrooms for brands like ING, Ticketmaster and WeTransfer. To see how these brands, and many more, do it head to pr.co/press-release-examples. You'll also see there what sort of images these brands make available with their announcements, along with how information is presented to make the journalist's job as easy as possible.

Own every media interview

Once you get more traction with your PR, you will – sooner or later – be interviewed by the media. It could be to add colour to a story you've pitched or to comment on a developing news story, or they may wish to profile you. However it comes about, it *will* come about. So check out the bonus skill builder – a guide to **Interview Skills** – at adamstones.co/influence. It covers how to be a simplifier not a complicator, how to appear confident and knowledgeable, how to 'bridge' away from tricky questions and how to flex your approach for print, online and broadcast media. Once you've learnt these skills, you'll be able to apply them to other areas, such as being on a discussion panel or fielding questions after a talk. It's a versatile – or rather *vital* – skill for your toolbox.

Handling crises & issues

It can take a long time to build a reputation but this can be stripped away by the media (and social media) in a matter of minutes. But... don't panic! That's rule one of PR crisis comms. The rest is all about smart planning and then open, agile response. I don't have the space to go into this topic in detail in this book, but here's a simple three step plan you can follow:

1. What might go wrong? What might present an issue or a crisis if it occurred – the actions of colleagues, flawed data, poor investments or faulty products? Make a note of these risks.

2. How can you prevent this? Note what you can do now to mitigate the chances of these things happening. You can prioritise mitigating actions by scoring scenarios according to the likelihood of them happening and how detrimental they'd be. Next, put these priority actions in place.

3. How would you respond? Consider what steps you'd take if a risk actually became a reality so you know the game plan and how you would communicate these actions.

If something does go wrong, get in fast and early to control the discourse. The communications must be from the person in charge, who must show empathy and outline exactly what they are doing to rectify the situation, even if that means admitting they don't have all the answers yet. Always be honest but focus on the solutions.

A leader will be on top of all the challenges they encounter and able to sail through because they have already identified where those troubles may emerge from. Use your communications skills to maintain a great reputation rather than drain your time and energy fixing a bad one.

/PR & MEDIA SUMMARY

BUILD A LIST: Keep a working list of media titles and contacts, clustered by type, with top targets highlighted. Keep it up to date and note all your interactions with these contacts. This list should also include stakeholders that have channels you can use.

BUILD RELATIONSHIPS: Ensure contacts are receptive to your future stories by making your value known, share useful information and opportunities, do favours, be a friend.

FOLLOW MEDIA CYCLES: After the initial news, there's reaction, commentary, analysis, features and further news. Understand this cycle to predict how you can jump in.

COMMENTATE: You don't just have to put out press releases, you can also issue short comments and make yourself available for interviews.

FIND YOUR STORY: When you do need to issue a story, ensure it is clear and relevant. Find the 'story in a sentence', three key messages and tick off the HWs.

BREADTH AND LENGTH: Before your story is even live, ensure you have already plotted its future – how you will extend it and repurpose it.

WRITE A RELEASE: Your press release should be succinct, informative and easy for the media to adapt. After a bold headline and powerful, summarising intro, get the essential info in up top. Include quotes.

PREP YOUR ASSETS: Your story may be supported by visuals, reports, infographics and spokespeople – ensure these are ready.

PITCH: A good pitch is personalised, making clear the relevance and significance of the approach. Never bcc, always tailor. Give them time to plan the story.

REVIEW: What worked and what needs improving? Which journalists are now in your book and need relationship building? Every activation requires a reflection.

/PUBLIC SPEAKING

There's an old Seinfeld joke that public speaking is feared by many people more than death, meaning that at a funeral you'd rather be the person in the casket than the one delivering the eulogy. So if this is you, you are not alone! But by building your competence in this area, you will soon come to love this crucial aspect of powerful communications – it's a hotline into people's hearts and minds, stirring their actions. When you thought of the leaders you admire, earlier in the book, chances are you were picturing them on stage, speaking to a crowd or room full of awed faces. And that's where you're heading.

The Ten Golden Rules of Public Speaking

Great talks and speeches can be the result of months of planning, drafting, editing and practicing. You might not have quite that time to prepare, but you should still not skip the steps because with them anyone can become a (frickin') awesome public speaker. These rules are built around giving a compelling presentation on stage, but you can apply the same approach to smaller talks such as presenting to teams or in pitches, to make them memorable and inspiring. Good luck and have fun.

1. Develop a kickass talk

The concept for a great talk starts with a single idea, a 'what if...' idea. It's the seed you want to plant in your audience that they'll then nurture and grow. TED describes this as your 'idea worth spreading' and this framing of 'passing the idea on' will help you to understand that your talk is not about you *asking* for something (requesting people change) but you *giving* something (offering a better future). As we've said, you are the guide, leading your hero along a path whose destination is that future. Along the way you will explain the challenges they face, the solutions to overcome these and give them the means and motivation to act.

So, what's your idea? Hopefully you will have a list of ideas in your content bank (see page 156) – something unique and wonderful, so we won't go over this again. Use the Killer Content chapter to **ensure you have one idea, three key messages and supporting information around each of these messages**.

Give it a structure: Sir Ken Robinson said he always followed a simple three-part structure in his talks and – because he delivered some of the most-watched TED talks of all time – you might want to do the same. Your three might be as simple as *challenge, solution and call to action* – either way, sketching a structure before drafting the speech is essential. Just as we humans all look different on the outside, beneath our skin there are very similar skeletons that enable us to function. Structure will ensure your talk is easy to follow and connect with for the audience, enabling it to perform *its* function. **(You can use the structure suggestions in the storytelling section to guide you.)**

Write it for the audience: As you write, you will flesh out your skeleton with stories, insights, evidence and humour (and we'll come on to this). But what you write must all be focused on one goal: deconstructing what your audience believes and then putting your idea in its place, using language and concepts they already understand to bridge the gap.

As always, you must understand who the audience is. What are their concerns and cares? As you will be placing your idea into their hearts and minds, you need to consider what they are already feeling and thinking. Naturally, a talk to a room of scientists will sound different to a talk to a group of CEOs – there will not only be structural differences but also completely different words and tones.

But do you really need to *write* a *speech*? For a TED / TEDx talk you may be asked to learn it by heart – if so, you *will* need to write your talk out in full. But even if you are not memorising it, you still need to know it well enough to speak with confidence. So, writing the full speech can help you know it is all covered (helping you to really examine what you will say). It also ensures you know exactly how long the talk is, which is important because if you ever over run, have to skip things or wrap up early, you will come across as unprofessional and uninspiring. But if writing in full feels constrictive to your natural, free style, at least script the opening and closing sections and note very detailed bullets within the middle section (noting key points and the nature of facts or anecdotes) to ensure you are at least following a plan.

'YOUR NUMBER-ONE MISSION AS A SPEAKER IS TO TAKE SOMETHING THAT MATTERS DEEPLY TO YOU AND TO REBUILD IT INSIDE THE MINDS OF YOUR LISTENERS.'
– CHRIS ANDERSON, *TED TALKS*

When you have your draft talk, go through it with an axe and chop away anything that is not serving a purpose. As Dorothy Sarnoff said, you need to finish speaking before the audience finishes listening – that's why TED caps talks at 18 minutes. Then, before it's final, practice delivering it to friendly faces such as colleagues. In this session, you want to hear if the talk is *technically* good; that it makes sense and achieves its ambitions. Ask for honest feedback and rework it if needed. You have to believe this talk is awesome if you want to convince others it is.

2. Rehearse & prepare

For some, memorising the whole speech and delivering it word for word is best (or even demanded) – it can give confidence in what you are about to say. But for others, merely memorising the structure and key points (or learning the talk and then allowing yourself to freestyle around the edges) will help deliver a better outcome because it can allow a more natural personality to come across.

If you are memorising, reading your speech over and over will never fully let it stick. Record your talk and listen back to it, speaking along as you do. Occasionally pause at random places to see if you can pick up the thread.

One big, massive no no is to read the speech on stage. You will totally lose your connection with the audience if you're not speaking from your heart to theirs. And you need eye contact to do this. If you are presenting by a laptop, you can of course have speaker notes to cue you on if needed. Otherwise, have some notes in your pocket – worst case scenario and you totally freeze, take a breath, find your place from your notes and pick it back up. The audience will be willing you to succeed so will be behind you if you do this.

Practice the delivery: Whether you're learning by heart or learning the heart of it, you need to practice *delivering* the speech. Once you feel ready, film yourself giving the talk. Watch it back, critique yourself and go again. Then get further insights on your delivery style with your first 'performance' – this should be back to those friendly faces who critiqued the structure. Here, you're looking for feedback on style: how you connect, your tone, your pace, your gestures... your *performance* (and more on building these aspects in the following rules).

The final prep: The big day has come. Make sure you're familiar with the room, with the layout and set up. Do you know what the tech is, are your slides working? If possible, go and stand in your spot and practice your opening, so you feel comfortable when the time comes.

'THERE ARE TWO TYPES OF SPEAKERS: THOSE WHO GET NERVOUS AND THOSE WHO ARE LIARS.' – MARK TWAIN

As you prepare to take the stage for real, nerves will be building – that's natural. The trick is to accept it and tap into this adrenaline to power up your performance. If you're feeling anxious then a few long, slow breaths will calm you and increase your optimism. And as Amy Cuddy suggests, you might even try carrying out some power poses backstage (see the Body Language section), using posture to create the mindset of someone who is about to blow the roof off. Which is, of course, what you will do next.

3. Start strong

You have 30 seconds to grab the audience's attention. Blow the opening and they're scrolling on Instagram, nail it and they're live streaming you. You may be familiar with the well-quoted parts of Martin Luther King's 'I have a dream' speech to 250,000 people in Washington, but did you know it starts: 'I am happy to join with you today in what will go down in history as the greatest demonstration for freedom in the history of our nation.' Boom. Imagine if this had been his opener instead: 'Right, there's lots of people here, some of you by the water, I see. So before I begin, just a few health and safety notices...'

Your opening remarks should grab the audience, giving them a reason to listen (the rules of AIDA – page 151 – totally apply here). You could try a **bold statement, story, enticing question or humorous observation**. Just cut the pleasantries and jump right in with something that disrupts their thinking – something original, bold or surprising – to force them to focus on you. This is not about giving everything away at the start – just a sense of what is to come.

Here are some strong openers from TED talks:

'Sadly, in the next 18 minutes when I do our chat, four Americans that are alive will be dead from the food that they eat.' – Jamie Oliver

'Imagine a big explosion as you climb through 3,000 ft. Imagine a plane full of smoke. Imagine an engine going clack, clack, clack, clack, clack, clack, clack. It sounds scary. Well I had a unique seat that day.' – Ric Elias

'OK, now I don't want to alarm anybody in this room, but it's just come to my attention that the person to your right is a liar.' – Pamela Meyer

4. Engage & connect

Now grow the audience connection through the talk. In the Body Language section, we learnt how to do this with eye contact, a smile and gestures that show meaning. Here are some other ways:

Tell stories: Harness everything we covered in the Storytelling section to weave in narratives and anecdotes. These will ignite emotions, create stronger bonds and help you connect on a *values* level, building rapport. But make them count – unless they bring colour and context to your idea they are wasting space.

Create tension: A great talk is full of tensions established by contrasting elements. We might contrast between what is and what could be, between challenges and solutions, contrast opposing views, display contrasting gestures or emotions, or we might show contrasting visuals. By sticking elements together as contrasts (especially when parts of those two elements mirror each other in some way – such as JFK's 'Ask not what your country can do for you, ask what you can do for your country'), we create a tension that not only holds attention but also, as we learnt earlier, opens the door for our idea to get in because we create a *desire* for it.

Signpost: Signal the direction the talk is heading in, using gestures to show you are moving on, even telling them what you are going to say before you say it, then recapping on what they have heard so the idea really sticks. Ask provocative questions that stir them and then go on to answer them immediately. Remember: you are the guide – you need everyone in the room to get to the destination but only you have the map.

Get a reaction: Laughter, clapping or cheers... any audible reaction will build engagement by bonding the audience to each other and to you, creating group endorsement for your idea. Humour also conveys that you are intelligent and likeable.

Mix it up: People will switch off if you maintain one style and pace throughout. You need to have parts that are slower, more serious, more funny or more interactive.

Respond: You should read the room and adjust your tone and approach subtly to account for how people are reacting. Do you need to lift the energy or tone it down? If people are disengaging, how can you adjust your style? As well-rehearsed as it is, your talk should feel like a one-off, only ever delivered in that place and time.

5. Posture, project, perform

At the heart of your talk is a performance. You are, after all, on a stage. Every word, movement and smile forms part of the theatrical production of your idea.

Think like an actor: Look at the emotional map of your talk and identify ways you can bring that emotion to life. Where can you add drama, where can you express the feelings of individual words? If a fact makes you angry then act angry. Say 'slowly' slowly, say 'curious' curiously. Do what you can to *show* what your words mean.

Don't rush: When nerves are high so is the tempo. Take a breath, relax and take your time. The word 'inspiration' has its roots in meaning 'breathing in' and you can use your breath to give yourself a pause and feel inspired as to what you want to focus on next. Slowing down shows confidence, and pauses will help your messages to stick, so don't fear them.

Know your performance habits: Everyone reacts subconsciously on stage in different ways – over expressive arms, a weird scratch, frequent ums and errs... The good news is everyone has them and they are all immensely fixable (a reminder why filming yourself rehearsing is important). If, like me, your quirk is a dry mouth, be confident to take a beat to take a sip. You can even work this into appropriate moments, such as when you need to allow the audience time to applaud that awesome joke (I still live in hope of that moment).

6. Be human

Being human is not at odds with performing – just the opposite, you need the performance to draw attention to your humanity.

Passion: Your passion makes your case persuasive, more so than your education or experience. Find the part of the story people can relate most to, or that means the most to you, and put your attention there.

Senses: When our senses are alive the experience becomes more vivid, activating memory cells and creating a more visual picture of the actions we will take after the talk. The audience's eyes and ears will be stimulated by your words and performance, but what about taste, smell, touch? Use images and descriptive language to trigger all the senses.

Vulnerability: Being able to show vulnerability in front of a group of people is a great strength. So, be honest. Share weaknesses you have overcome, or lessons you learnt through failures to build empathy and trust. If you watch Amy Cuddy's TED talk (see later), you'll find yourself trying not to shed a tear when she cries and the effect of her vulnerability is powerful – as the emotion builds like a wave, her idea rides it like a surfer into your heart.

Make mistakes: It's important to know that things probably will go wrong and that this is OK. When director Michael Bay was helping to launch a new Samsung TV, the autocue broke. Bay became agitated at not knowing what to say and walked off stage. The strange scene was played out on numerous media outlets with both Bay and Samsung's reputations being bashed. Just keep your cool, make a joke of it and press on.

Be mindful: Every speaker will get distracted by either real things – someone coughing or a microphone dropping – or just thought intrusions, like 'Uh oh, my ex is in the audience'. But at each intrusion you must treat them as if they are just leaves floating by on a stream, not issues that need to be examined. You already have a job to do so focus on that.

'THE ONLY REASON TO GIVE A SPEECH IS TO CHANGE THE WORLD.'

– JOHN F. KENNEDY

7. Simplify & visualise

A 15-to-20-minute talk will contain a lot of information. How much do you think the audience will realistically absorb after one listen? They'll remember the big moments and how they felt but not all the details. So don't overwhelm them with complexity – make sure the talk is easy to understand and act on.

Simplify words: Speak in words the audience will understand, not djargon (has that word stuck yet?). Explain complex ideas, use metaphors. Always ask yourself, 'Will the audience get it?' Simple words and sentences will also ensure you can construct soundbites – fully formed phrases the audience can quote you on and share on social media.

Explain numbers: Numbers can be hard to grasp in isolation so determine how to use context or comparisons to make them relatable (like how Jamie Oliver did earlier). If you have dense or data-heavy information you don't want to lose, you can always put this online and refer to where people can find it in the talk.

Use visuals: You are probably well aware of the phrase 'death by PowerPoint': a talk or presentation led by slides will kill the idea. Instead, any slides you need should play a supporting role and should be mainly visual. Any words you use should be minimal, to pull out a key word or phrase. You do not want people reading while you are talking – neither information source will sink in. And definitely avoid using bullets in slides – as TED's Chris Anderson says, bullets belong in *The Godfather*.

Sometimes the strongest slides are just one image, emphasising one point or the emotional qualities of your message. This also makes the message more memorable. Carmine Gallo, author of *Talk like TED* says, 'If you hear information delivered verbally, you are likely to remember about 10 per cent of that information three days later. Add a picture, however, and your recall rate will soar to 65 per cent.'

Use props: Hans Rosling's TED talks are famous for how he visualises his ideas. Talking about changes in population size and wealth over time, he presented an animated visual graph that he danced around and pointed at as it moved. It made the talk fun and memorable. In another talk, he simply stacked and moved boxes along a table to show the same changes. The use of this prop in a new way and his enthusiasm for it made the topic truly gripping. (His talk is listed later.)

8. Give them a STAR

Setting out to do a talk means having big ambitions – you will try to make people dream and change the way they behave, all in a short period of time. And to achieve this while competing with so many other options for content, you have to truly stand out.

To create this secret spice, Nancy Duarte, author of the brilliant guide to presentations, *Resonate*, uses the acronym **STAR: Something They'll Always Remember**. It's a moment where you drive your big idea home in such an awesome way, people just want to keep talking about it. And she describes five ways to create a STAR moment:

1. Memorable dramatisations (such as using a prop or acting something out)

2. Repeatable soundbites (these are easy to use in headlines or social media calls to action)

3. Evocative visuals (for an unforgettable emotional connection)

4. Emotive storytelling (stories connected to ideas are easier to share)

5. Shocking statistics (let them shock, don't rush past things that deserve attention)

You'll notice that these five ways are all contained within the other rules we've been through – it's up to you which you use to make your STAR moment but, however you do it, make sure you do do it. Being novel or exciting triggers dopamine, which is essential in establishing memories.

Duarte gives the following example... When Bill Gates did a TED talk on malaria, he wanted the audience to understand what it is like to live with the constant threat of this disease. 'There's no reason only poor people should have the experience,' he said. And then came his STAR moment – he opened a jar of mosquitoes and set them free amongst the audience. OK, they weren't carrying malaria, but the action instantly connected the audience with the idea, made it memorable and certainly got people talking.

9. Big finish

The end of your talk is where you deliver on the promise you established at the start. You asked a question, shared a fact or told a story, and now you need to close off in a way that echoes that start with a neat end and a positive resolution.

The end is also where you send your audience out into the world to *act* on your idea. You have to give them something to do with the desire you've been building – you have to give them a call to action, a call to be *heroes*. So, close by reminding the audience how awesome it will be once your idea is adopted and how they can make that happen. Kaboom.

10. What's next?

It's not time for the mic drop just yet. I think I see someone's hand raised at the back... Unless you are doing a TED-style talk and will be ushered off the stage as soon as time is up, you have to be prepared for questions.

Before the talk, imagine the type of questions you may get asked and have responses ready to roll. And if there's time set aside for questions and no one raises an arm, don't wait awkwardly, just rattle off one of your prepared answers by joking, 'You know, I often get asked... and I tell them...' This is also a great way to use material you had to cut from your talk. And once you have broken the stalemate, people will lose their inhibition and start firing more questions.

If you receive tricky questions, don't try to go on the defensive. Be honest if you don't know, or turn it back to them to clarify, expand or explain the reasoning for the question – there may be something in their reply that you can get stuck into.

OK, now the talk is done – you still have work to do. Firstly, how will you help the audience to act? You gave them a mission – ensure it is easy for anyone who watches your talk to connect with you, to get further information on your ideas and to *join your tribe*. Secondly, with this talk you now have some great content you could repurpose – you could pitch the idea for the talk somewhere else or split it up into smaller thought leadership pieces or short video content. Just don't let it go to waste.

Must see

Watching and studying great speeches, talks and presentations can help you see how the rules are used. Martin Luther King's 'I have a dream' speech has come up a few times already. It works because he hits so many golden rules – he presents the problem, the solution and the call to action. He tells stories, he makes it personal, he speaks to the individual in a crowd of over 250,000 people. He repeats key emotional ideas, saying the phrase 'I have a dream' eight times. And its firework ending just makes your heart thump in your chest and makes you want to *do different*. But fundamentally, it succeeds because he puts the why at the heart of it, the passion of his purpose. As Simon Sinek puts it, it's the 'I have a dream' speech, not the 'I have a plan' speech.

Check out these TED talks:

How great leaders inspire action – Simon Sinek
Do schools kill creativity? – Sir Ken Robinson
Your body language may shape who you are – Amy Cuddy
The best stats you've ever seen – Hans Rosling

And these speeches:

Malala Yousafzai's Address at the UN Youth Takeover
Barack Obama's Election Victory Speech
Martin Luther King's 'I Have a Dream' Speech

Bag a speaker spot

The opportunities to get started are all around – not only are there countless events and conferences to speak at but you can also just film yourself and upload it straight to social media. You can go from idea to Internet to tribe-building in an hour or two. But let's perhaps slow it down just a little and start by looking for the 'low hanging fruit' – the networks you are active in that you can contribute to most easily – and build from there. And note that some events may just be looking for a panellist to discuss a topic with authority, rather than a platform speaker. Don't overlook these as they will build your confidence and grow your network amongst other influencers.

Apply: Some big events will have a speaker application process listed on their website. Make sure you clearly express your talk idea and why this is a uniquely valuable contribution to the event.

Ask: If it's not listed, don't be afraid to ask what their application process is. There may be one person working in the background to curate the speakers and panellists – find out who it is and get to know them. Otherwise, just get your pitch together and apply as you would above, making it targeted and persuasive.

Associate: When you attend an event you'd like to speak at, introduce yourself to one of the organisers. Grow that connection over time and help them want to book you for a future event.

You probably already have your sights on speaking at a TEDx. They follow strict standards and are highly regarded, so speaking at one is a great calling card. And there's probably one happening soon in your area (geographically or sector-wise). From TED.com, follow the links to find relevant events.

You might also consider organising your own event. Bring your network together to develop an idea for a one off or regular event that showcases the best of your talents and adds value for your audiences. Use your combined marketing might to get people to sign up. And call in favours to bag a few headliners if needed. Just don't be afraid to start somewhere.

TO DO: Create a dedicated speaker sheet, a sort of 'why me' one pager that can accompany a pitch to speak at an event, and that's always ready to send out. This should include photos / videos from previous speaking events, testimonials and your bio.

/PUBLIC SPEAKING SUMMARY

DEVELOP A KICKASS TALK: Take your big idea. Build three key messages and supporting points around this and place it all in a narrative three act structure (e.g. *challenge, solution* and *action*) with a big opening and close.

REHEARSE & PREPARE: Off by heart or from the heart? You decide. But ensure you *really* know the talk. Film yourself and get honest feedback, then ensure everything is set up on the day.

START STRONG: You have 30 seconds to wow them or lose them. Jump right in and ignite curiosity with either bold statements, stories or questions.

ENGAGE & CONNECT: Make a strong *human* connection from the start using anecdotes, eye contact and humour. Don't forget to smile!

PERFORM: Body language and posture, tone and pacing – everything you do contributes to the *performance* of your talk. This all conveys the meaning of your words, keeping people captivated.

BE HUMAN: You are passionate about this so let it show. Stir all their senses to make it really memorable. Show your vulnerability to make a deeper connection.

SIMPLIFY & VISUALISE: Build up complex ideas using simple words and concepts. Use visuals where they complement your words. Consider what props can show off the message.

CREATE A STAR: Leave them with Something They'll Always Remember. This might be a dramatisation, a repeatable soundbite, an evocative visual, an emotive story or shocking stat.

BIG FINISH: Close off neatly, reflecting your opener. Remind people how awesome things will be if your idea is adopted and make sure they know what to do.

WHAT'S NEXT: Prepare for questions so there are no surprises and you remain in control. Once the talk is live then promote, repurpose and reflect.

ONWAR

/TO THE FUTURE

There's been a lot to go through, work out and practice in this book so congratulations for everything you've put in. When we started this journey, we looked at the Five Traits of Influence. We've walked through each of these step by step to allow you to apply them yourself – to supersize your influence, to work towards your intention.

Here's a quick recap of what you've achieved:

- ✔ **PURPOSEFUL:** Identified your driving purpose and ways to meaningfully bring this to life with authentic action.
- ✔ **PERSONAL:** Got to really know your audiences for this purpose – what they need and what you can offer – as well as who will help you along the way.
- ✔ **DISTINCT:** Built a kickass brand to take to these audiences using your *promise* and *personality* to shift their *perception*.
- ✔ **ACTIVE:** Learnt the fundamental behaviour change principles and formed a strategic plan to leverage your brand to achieve your change ambitions.
- ✔ **SKILLED:** Developed the essential communications skills needed to make your plan a success and achieve *influence*.

If you haven't already, try and fill in as much of the canvas as possible. Then stick it on the wall, nod to yourself smugly and then come back to it for occasional inspiration. Try to also give it a total refresh once a year.

Now it's time to fly

It's now time to apply all this knowledge. And the best way to do this is to just get going. Don't wait until it's perfect, until you have nailed everything, just try it out. Think of a comedian telling a joke on stage that *everyone* laughs at. She's probably told that joke hundreds of times, to different people, constantly refining it by sensing what was working and what needed work. In fact, the first time she told the joke, it probably totally sucked. It's only a killer joke now because she kept going until it was *connecting* with the audience. You also have to test your ideas out. Don't be afraid to make mistakes. Because that's how you learn. **The greatest risk in life is not to try.**

And continue to grow

Communication is a skill you cultivate, a muscle you work out. According to one stat, CEOs tend to read 4 to 5 books a month. Like 92% of facts, that one is made up but there is truth in the point that to achieve your goals you must keep learning and developing. Always be a student of your own industry – no matter how established you become – to really understand where it is going and where you can contribute or lead. Seek out the opportunities to learn new trends, and become confident in new principles. Keep flicking back over this book, scribble in it, doodle, pull it out and skim a chapter summary before a talk or writing task. This is your go-to communications companion.

What would Shakespeare do?

I also encourage you to do as much self-study as you can, acting like your own teacher. One way to do that is to apply what old Will Shakespeare describes as 'see things feelingly'. That means really inquiring mindfully into the world around you – try and understand *how* and *why* your senses are being stimulated. When you see communications that grab you – whether a speech or Instagram ad or anything else – how did it work? What magic trick have they pulled on you? What processes have been applied by the communicator to *influence* you? And when you see something that looks, well, crap, where did the communicator go wrong? Which of the lessons in this book have they ignored? A way to remember to do this is to ***read like a writer and listen like a speaker***. Do this for a variety of sources, not just from your usual channels, as ensuring a diversity of inputs will diversify your skills.

Strive for balance with *Control Goal Soul*

Flying, growing, getting all Shakespearey... it's going to take effort to achieve these goals and it's important to have this ambition. But you won't achieve these fully unless you maintain balance in your life. In 2020, when the world flipped upside down, many of us (myself included) struggled to know how to maintain healthy bodies and minds while juggling the demands of work and personal life. I worked with a fellow purpose-focused strategist, Gareth Jones, to develop a free tool anyone can use to **find balance and greater resilience** to achieve their ambitions. It's called Control Goal Soul because it identifies how all the essential ingredients that will determine the course of your life can be boiled down to three core areas: things over which we need to take *control*, things that provide a motivating *goal* and things that nurture our *soul*. It's important to support *each* area and get them to work together. The tool walks you through how to map these ingredients and then take command of them in your everyday life. It's free and I encourage you to check it out at **controlgoalsoul.com**

Thank you

The world has never needed you, your passion and your ideas more than it does right now. Thank you for making the commitment to go on this journey, to use powerful communications for positive change. I look forward to hearing your experiences of applying this book. And don't forget to share your knowledge with your peers – the more changemakers we can tool-up, the greater transformation we will achieve together.

'REMEMBER THAT A BETTER WORLD IS ALWAYS POSSIBLE. WE CAN TAKE BREAKS. WE CAN ENDURE SETBACKS. BUT WE CAN NEVER, EVER GIVE UP. YOU WERE BORN JUST IN TIME TO TRANSFORM THE WORLD.' – ERIC HOLTHAUS

//////////////////////////////////

/Bookshelf

There are many great books that have helped shape my thinking and approach. If you want to explore any of the ideas in this book in more detail, then these might help.

Better Business Writing by Bryan Garner
Brand the Change by Anne Miltenburg
Building a StoryBrand by Donald Miller
Communication Skills Training by Ian Tuhovsky
Do Story by Bobette Buster
Everybody Writes by Ann Handley
Influence: The Psychology of Persuasion by Robert Cialdini
Pitching Ideas by Jeroen Van Geel
Resonate by Nancy Duarte
Talk Like TED by Carmine Gallo
The Emotionally Intelligent Office by The School of Life
Tribes by Seth Godin
TED Talks by Chris Anderson
Valuable Content Marketing by Sonja Jefferson and Sharon Tanton

/Skills & Tools

There are a bunch of resources on the website for you to check out, including:

Book tools

The tools in the book can be viewed (some with working examples and guidance) and downloaded as templates. This includes: **Purpose Finder, Audience Profile Builder, Brand Archetype Finder, Communications Planners, Impact Auditor, and the** Influence Canvas.

Bonus skills

Some skills stand the test of time and those are the ones I've focused on in this book. Others – that evolve and change more rapidly – can be found on the website. This includes: **Interview Skills** (how to prepare for and deliver outstanding media interviews), **Social Media Skills** (how to build and activate your online tribe), **Networking Skills** (how to grow your influence in networks and at events, acknowledging how this is playing out digitally).

The website also has articles and exercises to help embed your new knowledge and skills, as well as extra material there simply wasn't space to cover here, including: **LinkedIn Profile Guide, Personality Types Guide, Ten Conversationalists to Avoid**. Additional resources will be regularly added. And if you have suggestions for what else you'd find useful, or have a completed canvas you'd like to share, please get in touch via the site. Good luck and have fun!

adamstones.co/influence

/About the author

Adam Stones is an award-winning writer and communications strategist working exclusively with people and brands making a positive impact. After several years in UK media (including with BBC Magazines and Telegraph Media Group), he then worked for two of London's leading communications agencies: Burson Cohn & Wolfe (PRovoke's Global Agency of the Year 2020) and Forster Communications (Consultancy of the Year 2021 at edie Sustainability Leaders Awards).

In 2016, he moved to Amsterdam and established the purpose-focused enterprise A'DAM Communications. He has helped organisations and individuals to find their voice, improve their skills and create deeper impact. Clients supported through his career range from global corporates to international charities, NGOs and governmental bodies, social enterprises and start-ups. He's also worked as the in-house Head of Communications for two purpose-led international organisations, BYCS and Metabolic.

He is the author of two other books: *And other stories*, a collection of short fiction; and *The Limey Project*, a cycling odyssey that hopes to encourage greater uptake of cycling, to improve the health and opportunities of people and places. This is a subject Adam actively advocates for and was the focus of his 2019 TEDx talk. He is a member of Impact Hub, a Fellow of the Royal Society of the Arts... and almost as good at Lego building as his two-year-old son.

adamstones.co
@adamstones